scale your everest

HOW TO BE A
RESILIENT ENTREPRENEUR

erik z. severinghaus

A POST HILL PRESS BOOK
ISBN: 978-1-64293-651-3
ISBN (eBook): 978-1-64293-652-0

Scale Your Everest:
How to be a Resilient Entrepreneur
© 2021 by Erik Z. Severinghaus
All Rights Reserved

Post Hill Press
New York • Nashville
posthillpress.com

Published in the United States of America
1 2 3 4 5 6 7 8 9 10

TABLE OF CONTENTS

What Will You Find at the Top of Your Everest?

Why do mountaineers climb mountains? As everyone knows, "because it's there." This famous, simple, and annoyingly accurate answer explains a lot about the mind of the mountaineer, a mind which may not be so different from the mind of the entrepreneur. From the "because it's there" perspective, mountaineers do not freely choose to climb the mountain. The reverse is often the case. They can't help it. They can't stop themselves. A mountain imposes itself upon the awareness of the mountaineer, a trigger is pulled, a chain of ideas, emotions, and events cascades through primitive limbic brainstem regions, higher-order explanations and excuses emerge, a vision is formed, an irresistible urge ensues, an overly optimistic plan soon follows, confidence is inflated, risks are ignored, and *kaboom*—an expedition is inevitable. Let's go! This will be awesome! A once-in-a-lifetime opportunity! Later, when they try to explain away the injuries and near-death experiences, the mountaineers produce a narrative that seems to make sense, but it doesn't truly capture the irresistibility of the call of the wild and the inevitability of the ascent when the idea first took shape.

Why do entrepreneurs start their businesses? Many researchers have studied this question, and their findings are not too surprising. A laundry list of motivations comprises the official description of why entrepreneurs do what they do. Instead of climbing the mountain "because it is there," entrepreneurs often start their businesses "because they can," or at least because they think they can. Motivations like independence, being in control, having enough autonomy to deploy wide-ranging skills and competencies, the quest for rewards (financial, social, status, self-esteem), dissatisfaction with the status quo, finding a path to personal fulfillment, and the desire to solve a problem or make an impact are all on the list. However—let's face it—ventures are to entrepreneurs as mountains are to mountaineers. The opportunity imposes itself upon the awareness of the entrepreneur, a trigger is pulled, a chain of ideas and emotions cascades through primitive brainstem centers, and then *kaboom*—the rest is history.

In *Scale Your Everest*, Erik Severinghaus shows us how his entrepreneurial passions got kindled and entrepreneurial ventures rolled out enough times for him to get beaten down, bounce back, lose and then make a fortune with lots of scars to show and lessons learned to share. To *our* great fortune, he shares these lessons with us from an elevated plateau with panoramic vistas that he reached after a recent exit. Erik imparts these hard-won insights for altruistic reasons. He wants to spare kindred spirits, up-and-coming entrepreneurs, and those who are already well along their trek to a distant summit, all of whom may face sudden death along the way, some of the pain and suffering he endured on his journey.

First, he helps builders identify and confront their blind spots, such as their signature trait of overconfidence, by encouraging them to abandon magical thinking and to prepare, prioritize, and adapt to ever-changing circumstances. Easy to say, difficult to do. To succeed, our mountain guide explains that mental resilience is required, which is achieved through exercising discernment, attaining inner stillness, being fully present, and having self-compassion and forgiveness of others. Add to this skill-building, strength-building, and a rigorous training program, and your odds of success increase. Along the way, you separate your personal identity from your business identity and let the air out of your inflated ego as you recognize being manipulated and exploited in your weaker, more naïve moments and how foolish some of your decisions and behaviors have been.

For the truly brave, Erik guides entrepreneur readers up the steep and treacherous icepack to a high ridge on the side of the mountain, from which one can look at the landscape at a distance and see everything in perspective. Here, he encourages entrepreneurs to develop self-awareness, including awareness about their own mental health. He explores issues like hypomania, anxiety, vulnerability to excessive bouts with drugs and alcohol—and he gets real about how these subterranean forces conspire to both shape and derail the intention and the execution of the entrepreneurial adventure. It's no secret that most entrepreneurs fail. While failure often results from factors beyond one's control (such as a nasty little pandemic that happens to shut down your supply chain while killing demand for your product and preventing your employees from doing their jobs), the DNA of the entrepreneur also has something to do with it.

How does entrepreneurial DNA relate to entrepreneurial motivation? Entrepreneurs who are motivated by "push" factors—things they don't like about their current situation—typically have worse business outcomes than those who are motivated by "pull" factors—an inspiration to create or contribute or to have an impact in a highly personal way. Like mountaineers who are inspired and lured by the pull of the mountain and the opportunity to join the hall of fame as they achieve their personal best, "pull" entrepreneurs are inspired and lured by their vision, their new venture idea, the overlap between their venture concept and their individual identity, and how the venture flows from a deeply personal sense of purpose. These are the entrepreneurs who are harder to deter. These are the entrepreneurs who slip more easily into heightened emotional states, deeper engagement with goals, flow states, and intense emotions while charismatically campaigning for their cause. Their visionary inspiration often corresponds to the mish-mash of mental health issues described by our mountain guide, and sorting this all out is part of the solution required to actually summit the entrepreneurial mountain.

Nice to know, and I would argue this is something you need to know as well. Our ambitious author deserves credit for putting this set of issues on the table. However, beyond the lessons learned and self-awareness applied, the existential question remains: what will you find at the top of your Everest? You envision the goal you seek to achieve with your business, and if you are one of the very few who actually summits the highest peak of mountain you set out to climb, then what? Typically, not what you were expecting. Big exits with rich rewards have their own problems, leading to a disturbing mental health condition called "sudden wealth syndrome," a disorienting, identity-crushing, disinhibiting reality distortion field that leads many entrepreneurs to unravel. Some flip out, some blow up their marriages, some become addicts, and some have been known to race their flashy new Maserati around a hairpin curve, lose control of their new, prized possession, and fly over an embankment to their tragic demise. And those who fall by the wayside before they reach the top of the mountain—the majority—how do they cope with the chronic stress and the financial devastation that accrues when they discover what they already knew, that Everest is notorious for avalanches?

This is the darkest entrepreneurship secret: those romanticized business outcomes that so many builders strive for usually don't achieve what they were intended to accomplish. The imagined results and the real results do not fully coincide. It turns out that, despite the hype, there is very little relationship between wealth and happiness. If you think that once you scale the summit of your Everest you will be flooded with happiness, joy, relief, fulfillment, and a sense of abundance, think again. That's a story line perpetuated by money-making Madison Avenue mythmakers who manufacture memes to mobilize our economy. The same applies to other hoped-for outcomes, such as love and family. It's often next to impossible to contain love, family, and entrepreneurship in the same vessel. Like so many adventures, the value of entrepreneurship lies in the journey itself, not the destination—which is often a letdown. I am fond of explaining that entrepreneurship is a social, emotional, cognitive, and behavioral practice. This practice, like other practices that lead to personal growth and development, forces us to confront our own vulnerability and fragility as people, and to recognize (and come to grips with) the mental health differences and demons that provoke disruptive and derailing social, emotional, cognitive, and behavioral symptoms when we are executing on our vision.

Hopefully, by the time you scale your Everest or get buried by an unanticipated avalanche along the way, you will have evolved through this book's lessons and the personal growth stages that make you fully ready to appreciate what you discover at the top. It's not a secret. At the top of your Everest is another trail that leads you somewhere else. In fact, not just one trail, but many routes and trails that go in many different directions, and nobody is there to tell you which one to pursue. Even though you achieved what you set out to accomplish, you still have to get down from the top of the mountain. Maybe you should have thought about that ahead of time? In any event, you are at the end of a climb, but you are still on the journey, and it's time to consolidate what you have learned as you determine how to proceed.

The lessons and skills conveyed by this inspiring book will help you along the way. If you are able to develop and mature as a person while you are on this adventure, by the time you reach your destination, you will be more capable of knowing what you truly want and what you truly need and asking for it. Your entrepreneurial expedition may lead to a summit or a bankruptcy or to a series of endeavors that on average work out or on average don't. Whatever the outcome, as you scale your Everest, you will learn that you have options when it comes to climbing the next mountain, and that the mountain you really want to climb may not be the one that imposes itself on your awareness.

Michael A. Freeman, M.D.
Founder, Econa
Clinical Professor of Psychiatry, U.C. San Francisco
School of Medicine
Mentor, The Entrepreneurship Center at UCSF

Why Mental Resilience Matters

A hero ventures forth from the world of common day into a region of supernatural wonder: fabulous forces are there encountered and a decisive victory is won: The hero comes back from this mysterious adventure with the power to bestow boons on his fellow man.

—Joseph Campbell,
The Hero With A Thousand Faces

As I stood on top of Mount Everest at 29,032 feet, I was running on fumes and low on oxygen. To make matters worse, I had herniated a disc in my spine so badly I could barely walk. I was behind schedule, moving slowly, and desperate to make it to the safety of Camp 2, known as "Advanced Base Camp." But I didn't make it, and I would instead need to spend another night in the "Death Zone."

In the middle of that night I woke up, freezing cold and gasping for breath. After a few minutes of confusion while I tried to figure out what was going on, I realized that the oxygen tank I was breathing from had run dry. And so, disoriented and struggling to breathe, I dragged myself to the edge of my tent and signaled for help. Mingma Sona, my climbing Sherpa, saved my life by changing out my oxygen tank as I lay in the tent, feeling weak and pathetic.

The next day, as I rappelled down the Lhotse face toward safety, I took a moment of silence as I watched the body bags of two less lucky climbers being lowered down the ropes next to me.

Climbing Mount Everest is the second hardest thing I have ever done. The second nearest I have ever felt to dying.

The first is being an entrepreneur.

I know that probably sounds like an exaggeration, and it certainly isn't the usual media narrative about entrepreneurs. In our present-day myths, entrepreneurs are celebrated as superheroes— modern-day alchemists who spin gold from their ideas, hard work, and perseverance. We are sometimes regarded as nerdier versions of celebrities, movie stars, or athletes.

Not quite.

The reality is much different, a trail of broke founders and broken companies. Most of us who have lived through the journey know that, but we bury that truth in places we don't talk about. Behind the bravado, entrepreneurs are a vulnerable population, with three times the rate of addiction and twice the rate of suicide of the general population.[1]

---

[1] This data comes from Dr. Michael Freeman's research "Are Entrepreneurs 'Touched With Fire'?" In this data, 5 percent of entrepreneurs and 2 percent of a control group self-reported a history of suicidality, and 12 percent of entrepreneurs and 4 percent of the control group reported substance abuse issues. There aren't nearly enough studies on this topic to know whether these numbers will be reproduced consistently, nor do we know which way the causality arrow goes. Does entrepreneurship induce these mental crises, or are people with mental challenges pre-disposed to entrepreneurship? While the data and explanations are sure to evolve over time, in the five years of researching and writing this book, I did not meet a single entrepreneur or mental health professional who disputes the notion that this is an industry in crisis.

When you think about it, the most influential ingredient for the success of the company is the effectiveness, the mind, of the entrepreneur. To beat the odds and succeed, we have to optimize our minds for things like situational awareness, decision-making under uncertainty, and anxiety management.

Sound easy?

Hardly. Few truly understand the entrepreneur's journey—the universal financial, emotional, and mental challenges. None of the books, classes, or incubators even try to develop the mental resilience and psychological strength for the toll that entrepreneurship takes. I know, because I have been through many of them.

I have had investors renege on deal terms and give me fake wire transfer numbers while assuring me the money I needed to avoid bankruptcy was on the way. I have watched trusted mentors rip off my business ideas and present them as their own. The journey has cost me an engagement, a best friend, a six-figure bank account, and probably more than a few years of my life.

I compensated for the hard times with too much booze and compulsive exercise (among other bad habits). The anxiety led me to my own personal and more terrifying "Death Zone," fearing I was having a heart attack at twenty-nine coupled with fantasies about jumping in front of the El train to make the pain go away.

These struggles might sound outlandish to the uninitiated, but they are common to the point of being cliché in the entrepreneurial community.

I count myself as one of the lucky ones, the "successful" ones. I was a middle-class kid who taught himself to program computers in second grade and always wanted to be an entrepreneur. I literally have been able to live my dream. In college at the University of North Carolina, I co-founded iContact, a company we sold for $189 million. Later, I helped take SpringCM to a $220 million exit. Along the way, I acquired a shelf full of entrepreneurial awards and recognition. The other side of the story is that I have a lot more failures than successes on my record. From both the ups and the downs, I have learned one thing:

To succeed as an entrepreneur requires resilience, but no one teaches entrepreneurial resilience.

Entrepreneurial innovation has been around for as long as humanity. The common threads of imagination and action connect builders, inventors, and entrepreneurs across continents and generations. Most of us viscerally understand the deep-seated feeling within our souls that we must build, create, and innovate. For us, entrepreneurship is an almost sacred journey to answer a call deep within ourselves to imagine what could be and move the world in that direction.

Philosophers, statisticians, and behavioral economists have spilled gallons of ink trying to understand why entrepreneurs do what we do. For those of us who answer the call that comes from deep in our souls, the answer is as obvious as it is difficult to explain. It would be like asking trees why they grow. It's what we are born to do. We often discovered this at a young age and found ourselves different than other kids. Our ambitions, our desires, our dreams. We feel the powerful draw to answer what Joseph Campbell termed "the call to adventure," regardless of what some egghead may tell us about the expected median risk-adjusted discounted cash flows of the profession.

And so, many of us answer the call of entrepreneurship without really even knowing what we are signing up for—even though we are too cocky to admit it. I certainly didn't know what lay ahead.

In the pique of excitement, we rarely stop to ask ourselves, "Is this what I want to do for the next eight years?" I never did that.... Buried deep in my arrogance was the idea that my company would surely be sold or IPO in half that time. And so we begin the journey. Along the way, we find ourselves disoriented when our sense of self seems somehow misaligned with how the world views us. Sometimes we struggle to understand why no one takes us seriously as entrepreneurs. Other times we wonder why everyone seems so certain we will succeed while we fight with self-doubt.

That disconnect leads to very real symptoms in our minds and bodies. Slowly, over time, our sleeping, eating, drinking, exercising, and socializing patterns change. Our mind responds in the way that it has evolved to respond, releasing chemicals into our bloodstream to prepare us for danger. Unfortunately, those defense mechanisms are poorly designed for the intellectual challenges we currently face and actually work against us.

This is only made worse by the advice that surrounds us. Most of what we hear and read about the entrepreneurial journey is filtered through the selection bias of only hearing the success stories or through messengers like venture capitalists (VCs) who benefit from entrepreneurial volatility. The bad advice only reinforces our notion that failure comes from weakness, "real" entrepreneurs are the ones who will always take on more risk. We become convinced that our success as human beings is dependent upon the financial success of a company.

Without realizing it, I fell victim to all of these dynamics, and they almost broke me. I made bad decisions as an entrepreneur and lost my shareholders' money. Even more troubling, I lost friendships and relationships, and I began fantasizing about ending it all through the only noble exit I could think of: taking my life rather than facing the consequences of my mistakes.

During this dark period, I found myself searching for some sort of a manual to understand my struggle and figure out how to deal with my situation. I knew it was unhealthy, but I couldn't figure out what the problem was or how to go about solving it. I found inspiring ideas and thoughts from different sources but couldn't find anything that pulled them together to address the entrepreneurial journey. I have since come to realize that I wasn't alone, and that tragically, entrepreneurs suffer addiction, depression, and suicidality among other mental health situations at rates far higher than the general population.

After I sold the company, I kept researching and learning. I wanted to understand why I had broken, how to improve myself, and how to help others. Gradually, when talking with entrepreneurs, I would admit to them the struggles I experienced and the insecurity I felt during the journey. I learned from their responses that it wasn't just me; in fact, every one of them had experienced the same feelings. And so, as I continued these conversations, I started trying to find ways to help.

I kept learning as I took on my next major challenge, trying to climb Mount Everest. A goal for more than ten years, I knew that mental resilience would be essential if I was going to make it to the top. I needed to be stronger mentally as a mountaineer than I had been as an entrepreneur. In climbing that literal mountain, I learned a tremendous amount about developing mental resilience that gave me even better perspective on the analogous challenges in entrepreneurship.

As I learned and taught, I developed a framework to help entrepreneurs train their minds for the journey with the goal of making entrepreneurship more successful and enjoyable. I discovered three essential skills for entrepreneurial resilience: the need to constantly prepare for challenges ahead, prioritize what is important, and adapt to ever-changing circumstances.

Those skills are easy enough to say, but as humans we have a number of blind spots that make them hard to do effectively and consistently. Digging deeper, I found four key abilities that enable those skills: discernment, stillness, presence, and forgiveness. These skills have been recognized by philosophers and doctors for millennia as essential to the human condition, but the deeper I went, the more I realized that they also form the foundation for effective entrepreneurship. Again, each of them is easy to say but can take a lifetime to develop.

And so, I developed a training regimen not unlike what I would use to run a marathon or climb a mountain to develop those abilities and skills. Specific, actionable exercises that can help develop these ethereal abilities.

To reverse the disheartening trends in entrepreneurial outcomes, we need to change the way we think about entrepreneurship. We need to put founders first and train them for the journey ahead. I hope this book will be the guidebook for others that I desperately needed in my darkest moments as an entrepreneur. I hope it helps you to take on this magical journey with greater success, happiness, and joy than I was equipped to do.

As we explore these ideas, I'll combine my own experiences with research to better contextualize the journey and challenges of the entrepreneur.[2] Once we have laid that foundation, we will go through specific activities to improve mental resilience and thus improve odds of success.

For each of these concepts, I'll relate my own stories and what I have learned in the process through my experience and research. I'll also share a story from Everest that helps me contextualize the lesson in another domain. This is a book about entrepreneurship, not mountaineering, but the two share so much in common that I think the lessons from Everest help reinforce the concepts. I'll also invite you to journal with specific prompts at the end of each chapter. These prompts can be done yourself on paper, or talked through with a therapist, trusted friend, or partner.

LESSON FROM MOUNT EVEREST

Ever since there have been mountaineers, there have been people who ask them why they climb. Why put yourself through discomfort and risk to stand on a high place?

---

2   Everyone experiences the entrepreneurial journey differently. We bring our own history, pre-conceived notions, and biases to everything we do, and entrepreneurship is no different. This is a deeply personal issue for me, and while my challenges and struggles are uniquely my own, at their root they are common across entrepreneurs. I'm a white guy who loves sports, wears baseball caps backward, and has been called the "epitome of heteronormative." If "tech-bro" were in a dictionary, my face could be next to it. I won't pretend that I have walked a mile in the shoes of other groups; the closest I get is vicariously as a supporter and investor. Female entrepreneurs and entrepreneurs of color in particular are doubtlessly going to have a different set of challenges and context for them. Addressing those particular struggles is important, but it is outside the scope of this book and my personal experience. And so, while acknowledging that I'm confined to my own set of life experiences, I try to present concepts and strategies that are universally applicable.

The mountaineer's cliché answer to why one climbs a mountain is to quote George Mallory, who famously answered the question, "Because it's there!" Tragically, Mallory died high atop Mount Everest, but his indomitable spirit lives on in every mountaineer.

I have used that quote plenty of times! I always appreciated it as a pithy response to a question that I never really wanted to explore too deeply. But even more than Mallory's quote, I loved the famous answer by Sir Edmund Hillary to a similar question, that "It is not the mountain we conquer, but ourselves." Quoting Mallory or Hillary gave me a reputable answer without having to actually search within myself to find my own perspective on the question.

The clichés worked well enough for me to explain climbing mountains like Kilimanjaro or Aconcagua, but as I prepared for Everest, I felt like I owed a deeper answer to the people in my life who loved me. Most of my closest friends and family were supportive of my trip to Everest. They understood it was a call to adventure that I needed to answer and did their best to help in any way they could. Some introduced me to other mountaineers for advice, others gave me good luck charms or gifts to help on the journey. Many came from across the country to see me off and wish me luck as I left for Nepal.

But that heartwarming response wasn't universal. There were others who thought my quest was selfish, indulgent, or just idiotic and weren't shy about letting me know. I don't know that I owed them an explanation, but I did feel like I owed it to myself to really think through and develop my own answer to the question. I never thought my answer would change their minds (spoiler alert: it didn't). Instead, I wanted to check myself and make sure I had deeply thought through why I was going to go through the danger, expense, and hardship that I knew would come. I also hoped that by putting my purpose in writing, I would be that much more committed when I got there and resilient to the challenges.

I took a longer take on "It is not the mountain you conquer, but yourself." I wrote the following poem to try to explore my motivations about the challenges and difficulties I have taken on. Writing it helped me understand that the goal of the journey was transforming myself and growing as a person enough to make it to the top.

"A Letter to Those Who Love Me"
Why do I need to go climb?
And why not a smaller mountain?

A soul can't be bought, it must be earned
It's not about "because it's there"
It's because I'm here.
I'm not trying to be George Mallory
I'm trying not to be Willie Lowman

I would literally not be me absent the
challenges of becoming an Eagle
Or Philmont
Or Ironman
Or Aconcagua
Or Simple Relevance
Or Papa Johns
And now Sagarmatha

These iterations of the hero's
journey have created me

Absent them, I'd be a different
soul in this sack of flesh
Less thoughtful, less kind. Less
confident. Less settled. Less joyful.
I would not want to be that man
Far more than death I fear life as the cold and
lonely soul who knows neither victory nor defeat

This isn't a journey to the top of a summit
It's not about standing atop the world
It's a journey inward
It's about the preparation far more than the test
Summit day is simply a celebration of
the transformation and preparation
that allows me to get there

Hubris may be a catalyst for bildungsroman
but is ultimately its antithesis

The highest and most powerful peak
surrounded by a spiritual mecca
I may be too fortunate to ever know
the strength and joy of the Sherpa
Too coddled and rich to know their wisdom
But perhaps I can commune
with them for a moment
Perhaps some amount of meditation and
arduousness in such a spiritual land

In the shadow of Mother Earth can
awaken and develop more of Erik

TAKEAWAY FOR ENTREPRENEURSHIP

I have had loved ones in my life respond to my entrepreneurial
ambitions with the same mixed feelings as my mountaineering
plans. Your loved ones are likely to have their concerns as well.
Understanding your motivations for the journey will help you be
happier during the process and more resilient to the challenges.

JOURNAL PROMPT

Why did you decide to be an entrepreneur? How do you expect
yourself to change as a result of this journey? Why leave a perfectly
good job? Why spend less time with your family? Why put your
family through financial risk to go on this journey?

Keeping Your Company Alive for Eight Years

Mountains should be climbed with as little effort as possible and without desire. The reality of your own nature should determine the speed. If you become restless, speed up. If you become winded, slow down. You climb the mountain in an equilibrium between restlessness and exhaustion. Then, when you're no longer thinking ahead, each footstep isn't just a means to an end but a unique event in itself.

—Robert M. Pirsig,
Zen and the Art of Motorcycle Maintenance

When people find out that I climbed Mount Everest I can usually expect to get one of three questions: Did you see any dead bodies? Yes. Tragically. Would you do it again? Maybe. For the right reasons. What's the key to getting to the top safely and successfully? The answer is more complicated.

In my experience, the underlying principles of success for mountaineering and entrepreneurship are really the same.

From a certain (reductionist) standpoint, climbing a mountain is pretty simple. To successfully climb a mountain, no matter the size, there are three basic steps:

- Stay Alive
- Don't Quit
- Keep Walking Up Hill

In a certain sense, you can apply the same rule to pretty much any endurance activity. Want to run a marathon? Same basic steps:

- Stay Alive
- Don't Quit
- Keep Moving Forward

The hard part of all of this is being resilient to the many problems that arise in the meantime. Entrepreneurship, in its most basic form, is no different. The odds are stacked against entrepreneurs and many forces conspire to put a company out of business. It's easy to get caught up in all of the problems we face every day. But, in the simplest possible way, our jobs as entrepreneurs are to keep ourselves and our businesses alive, resist the urge to quit, and keep moving forward until we find a way to succeed. Research shows that the median successful exit is about seven to nine years (depending on industry).[3] At a fundamental level, the key to entrepreneurship is figuring out how to keep moving forward for eight years—how to be resilient.

It may seem obvious, but these steps are listed in order of importance, and "stay alive" is first for a reason. Not just metaphorically (keeping your business alive)—literally. Take care of yourself as a

---

3   Abdullah, Sammy. "How Long Does It Take A Startup To Exit?" Crunchbase. November 25, 2018. https://about.crunchbase.com/blog/startup-exit.

human being first. Only then can you focus on keeping the company functioning and then continuing to execute on the plan. This sounds obvious, right? In order for the company to keep executing, the company has to survive. In order for the company to survive, the entrepreneur has to survive. All the tools of entrepreneurship are useless if the carpenter is in the middle of a nervous breakdown. It's like Maslow's Hierarchy of Needs applied to the world of the entrepreneur.[4] Tautological. Duh. No shit, Sherlock.

But, like so many blindingly simple ideas, I learned from experience that this one is easy to forget. I spent so much time and energy focusing on daily activity that I lost sight of the simple philosophy above. I got my priorities all mixed up.

I was fluent in customer blueprints, agile development, crossing the chasm, and dozens of other frameworks to move the business forward. But I couldn't see the forest for the trees. I spent so much time trying to optimize my cap table to maximize my theoretical future returns that I forgot to make sure I had enough money to ensure that we wouldn't need to quit. And as the pressure to quit became overwhelming, I spent so much time and emotional energy trying to figure out how to keep our company solvent that I forgot to focus on keeping myself alive and functioning at a high level. I lost sight of the blindingly obvious steps: stay alive, don't quit, and keep moving forward.

I focused on the priorities above in reverse order, a mistake that cost my investors and me a lot of money. It was nearly much worse; my lack of preparedness and adaptability could have cost me my

---

4   Maslow, A. H. "A Theory of Human Motivation." Classics in the History of Psychology. Originally Published in *Psychological Review* (1943): 370-396. http://psychclassics.yorku.ca/Maslow/motivation.htm.

health or even my life. The entrepreneurial journey has tragically claimed too many promising lives far too early.

I wasn't prepared for the worst days. Losing track of these priorities meant that I didn't have the cash to weather a downturn and had to exit on unfavorable terms. And those pressures only added to the psychological strain as dangerous symptoms started to present themselves. In the darkest moments, I had a lot of suicidal thoughts and fantasies that I thankfully avoided acting on. I still get a pit in my stomach when I think about how far down that path I actually was.

This idea that you need to prepare yourself for an eight-year journey is present under our noses in lots of research, but rarely if ever is brought up in the typical entrepreneurial advice talk. The $13 billion entrepreneurial advice industry has grown exponentially, but it is full of charlatans peddling snake oil. Incubators, books, films, TED talks, university courses, and countless other programs exist to try to make a buck off of the act of coaching and preparing entrepreneurs. But, for all the advice on the topic, precious little focus is put on helping entrepreneurs prepare themselves mentally for the tour of duty they are signing up for.

Successful entrepreneurs like to attribute their successes to their heroism rather than the more likely combination of longevity and luck. When you listen to successful entrepreneurs speak, they tend to offer the same keys to success. You'll usually hear some combination of "grit," "determination," and "never take no for an answer." No question about it, succeeding as an entrepreneur requires grit, determination, strength, and smarts. But success requires more, and the all-important mental aspects are all too often left out of the conversation.

Chances are you rarely hear failed entrepreneurs speak about their ventures. Panels for audiences are constructed to sell tickets, and people (wrongly) believe they can learn a lot more from those who succeeded than those who failed. And so, your head will be filled with stories that are more a product of survivorship bias than actual analysis. If you get to know a number of failed entrepreneurs, you'll see that most of them also possess grit, determination, strength, and smarts. Oftentimes, they just didn't get as lucky. Put another way, they weren't resilient to the stresses of entrepreneurship long enough to get lucky.

It may seem obvious in hindsight which entrepreneurs will survive for those eight-plus years and succeed, but actually predicting that success is a fool's errand. Given the billions of dollars at stake in venture capital decisions, you can be sure that if there were some traits that differentiated the successful entrepreneurs from the unsuccessful, venture capitalists (VCs) would be using that knowledge to make decisions. Spoiler alert: no such test exists, and so venture capital continues to underperform as an asset class.

Grit, determination, smarts, and all the rest are absolutely required to succeed as an entrepreneur. Without a doubt, they are necessary. But they also aren't sufficient. Every entrepreneurial success story also contains a tremendous amount of luck—an existential truth that honest entrepreneurs will admit (the insecure ones never will; they need every win to validate their greatness). This leads to the natural question—how do you increase your chances to "be lucky?"

Let's look at the eight years another way. Entrepreneurship is like a game of chance where the odds of winning are low, but the payoff, if you succeed, is exponential. I'll use a more common game of chance to illustrate.

Entrepreneurship as Roulette

Imagine a high-rollers game of roulette where the minimum bet is ten thousand dollars per spin but correctly guessing the number where the ball lands pays off a cool million. Since there are thirty-eight numbers on a typical (double zero) roulette wheel, these are fantastic odds! You have a one in thirty-eight chance for a one hundred times payout.

But of course, there's a catch. In my made-up roulette game with great odds, you have to put your ten thousand dollar bet all on a single number; you can't spread out your bet. So, if you sit down at the table with forty thousand dollars, you only get four spins to hit your number. Even though your payoff-adjusted odds are favorable, about 90 percent of the time you'll lose your entire forty thousand dollars! You don't have enough spins to take advantage of the fact that the game should be very lucrative.

About 10 percent of the time, you will hit your number and walk away having made a million dollars. It's a high-risk game; you're far more likely to go broke than to win, but if you can stay alive long enough, the payoff is exponential. In this admittedly contrived scenario, the key to winning is staying alive long enough to get lucky.

In our roulette example, you have two theoretical ways to improve the odds to collect your payout:

Option one is to figure out how to get better at playing roulette; that is, to become more skilled at picking numbers. Maybe you study the pattern of numbers that come up historically, hoping for some small inconsistency in the wheel. There actually is some evidence that with enough time, energy, and computer modeling power, you might be able to improve your chances a bit.[5] But it's almost impossible to become so good at picking numbers that you fundamentally change the odds by very much. You're trying to predict outcomes in a complex and dynamic system, much of which is out of your control.

Option two is to figure out how to get more than four spins, how to be more resilient to bad luck. Staying alive longer has a huge impact on your odds of hitting the jackpot! Maybe you bring more money to the table; with a bankroll of eighty thousand dollars, you can take eight spins, and your odds of winning go from 10 percent to about 20 percent. Bring two hundred and fifty thousand dollars and you'll now have twenty-five spins. The odds are about 50 percent that you'll walk away with the million. Improving your chances of winning is all about improving your resiliency to bad fortune and allowing yourself to stay in the game long enough to hit the jackpot.

This book is all about option two. Being resilient, staying in the game longer, and giving yourself better odds to eventually be lucky. There are financial strategies that come from this mindset (raise more money, spend less money, extend your ability to stay alive as a company). But the most important key to resilience comes from preparing yourself mentally and psychologically for the journey ahead.

The point of this example is that for games where success is unlikely but the payoff is exponential, you need to focus your energy on a strategy to stay in the game as long as possible. Figuring out how to get more spins is both easier and more likely to be effec-

---

5   Knapp, Alex. "Scientists Beat The House At Roulette With Chaos Theory." *Forbes*. October 27, 2012. https://www.forbes.com/sites/alexknapp/2012/10/27/scientists-beat-the-house-at-roulette-with-chaos-theory/#7b4160d7710d.

tive than figuring out how to beat the odds by becoming better at roulette.

Entrepreneurship has many of the same characteristics. While we want to believe that we make our own luck, there are far more factors outside than inside our span of control in the dynamic system of entrepreneurial success. Decisions by partners, competitors, the press, and VCs can make or break the journey and are oftentimes driven by unseen influences. What we like to think of as a nice, simple, deterministic system that depends on the personal qualities of the entrepreneur is actually more akin to chaos theory, where imperceptible differences in the structure of the roulette wheel lead to wildly different outcomes in terms of where the ball lands.

And yet, almost everyone who gives you entrepreneurial advice will focus on how to play roulette better, not how to stay in the game longer. This appeals to the natural human desire for agency and the hope that our destiny is under our control. In my experience, the best entrepreneurs are the exception to the rule: they are the few that understand how much of their future is outside their control. To paraphrase the Serenity Prayer, they focus on changing what they can, accepting what they can't, and developing the wisdom to know the difference.

These entrepreneurs, the ones who focus their energy on the resilience they need to survive long enough, recognize that luck is a big part of the process, and so they figure out how to stay in the game long enough to get lucky. To have a competitor go out of business. To see the market shift. To get that unlikely reference customer or business development channel. To add the killer feature that becomes a differentiator they didn't realize.

The research shows that it usually takes at least eight years of hard work to get lucky.[6]

The hardest part is figuring out how to stay in the game that long. Imagine where you were as a person eight years ago. Think about where you can expect to be eight years from now. Think of all the changes likely to happen in your life. Think of the changes that are certain to happen to society in that time. Two presidential elections, wars, pandemics, regulatory changes, technology disruptions. The world is certain to be a very different place in eight years' time.

While there's no shame in stepping aside as a founder when you realize that other leadership can be better for the organization, most of us dream of maintaining leadership in the company when the vision is ultimately realized. And so, the fundamental and most important job of the entrepreneur is to keep the company alive long enough to get lucky and succeed while also preparing yourself to lead the organization effectively and endure the strain of entrepreneurship for at least the expected eight-year endurance run.

To add to the frustration, your progress along the eight-year journey won't be linear. There are a lot of ups and downs. Often you'll feel like you're going backward. Preparing yourself for the journey isn't about being effective on the average day. What will matter is how you show up on the worst day of the worst month. It's the day that feels like it should be in a sad country song, when nothing is going right with your truck, family, investors, or customers.

---

6   Hathaway, Ian. "Time to Exit." Ian Hathaway. January 9, 2019. http://www.ian hathaway.org/blog/2019/1/9/time-to-exit. Abdullah, Sammy. "How Long Does It Take A Startup To Exit?" Crunchbase. November 25, 2018. https://about.crunch base.com/blog/startup-exit/. Bowden, Adley. "VC Investing Still Strong Even as Median Time to Exit Reaches 8.2 Years." VentureBeat, Inc. May 19, 2017. https://venturebeat.com/2017/05/19/vc-investing-still-strong-even-as-median-time-to-exit-reaches-8-2-years/.

Leading effectively during that time is the crux of the challenge of being an entrepreneur. It's hard to last eight years in the grinder. It's hard to keep finding the money to keep going. It's hard to come to grips with the mistakes you make during that time. It's hard to stay motivated behind an idea. It's hard to evangelize to your investors, partners, and employees for that long and still believe in yourself. Winning this race is a marathon, not a sprint.

The good news is that the skills needed to build the mental resilience to succeed as an entrepreneur are no different than for other situations. The entrepreneur's journey is just a magnified and extremely intense version of the human journey. Decision-making in stressful circumstances, survival mentality, leadership under duress, and other similar topics have been studied, debated, and written about since time immemorial.

The goal of this book is to provide you with a training plan to maximize your execution time as an entrepreneur. To teach you how to prepare to sit down at the roulette wheel and be ready for the pressure so you get more spins, more chances to get lucky. In doing so, I'll adapt principles from systems theory, probability theory, psychology, philosophy, comparative mythology, evolutionary biology, and other disciplines. When you're done reading, I'm confident you'll have a framework for understanding and a set of tools that will allow you to survive and thrive for much longer amid the pressure of the entrepreneurial journey.

LESSON FROM MOUNT EVEREST

It's probably no coincidence that it also took me a little longer than eight years to climb Mount Everest. In fact, the preparation took ten years, the climbing took ten weeks, and I spent ten minutes at the top of the world.

During those ten years of training, the physical workouts were punishing. I had to completely change my body, building strength and endurance. My gym workouts as I got close to leaving for Nepal lasted eight to ten hours. I also had to learn a lot about the technical art of mountaineering. I was determined not to be one of the newbies showing up to Everest needing a tutorial on how to put on my crampons. Part of that was for safety, and a big part was for pride. I wanted to show up to Everest and feel like I belonged on the mountain. I wanted the mountain to accept me and let me summit. I didn't want to show up arrogantly expecting to complete the journey without having put in the work.

In the months before I left for Nepal, I spent a lot of time in Colorado. One of my closest friends, Aaron Houghton, had recently moved to Boulder, which gave me the perfect base of operations to train at altitude and get out to the mountains.[7] Aaron and I would skin up the Minturn Mile to the top of Vail one day, and I'd go ice climbing with my girlfriend the next.[8] I was having a blast and pushing myself to new limits physically every day.

Aaron asked me one day about my training plan, and he was surprised to hear that I had an hour of meditation and visualization each day as part of my actual Everest training plan. While I was doing everything I could to get my body, muscles, and lungs ready for the stress I knew I would put on them, I also expected that training my mind would be just as important.

As I built my physical training plan, I also developed a parallel mental training plan for the mountain. I read a number of books

---

7   Aaron and I have been close friends and co-founders for years. He has also started a community focused on founder mental health called Founders First. I recommend checking it out. https://www.foundersfirstsystem.com/.

8   More information about this legendary run can be found at http:// www.minturnsaloon.com/minturn-mile.html.

on the concept, developed meditation and visualization routines, and made sure to incorporate mental resilience as a key tenant of the preparation.

I made a ton of mistakes during the trip. My body almost failed me. My will to continue hit its limit. Most seasoned mountaineers don't make it to the top of Everest on their first attempt, and I'm incredibly fortunate to have done so. I have absolutely no doubt that the mental training and intentional development of resilience was critical to that success. I knew I had a long and arduous journey ahead of me, and I did my best to prepare my mind for that reality.

TAKEAWAY FOR ENTREPRENEURSHIP

Entrepreneurship and mountaineering are both endurance runs against the odds. Preparing your mind for the journey through practice and training will increase the time you can stay in the game and dramatically improve your odds of succeeding.

JOURNAL PROMPT

Visualize yourself in eight years' time.

Where do you live? What city? What neighborhood? What type of home?

What is your family like? Are you married? Do you have children? Are they still at home?

What are your finances like?

What is your company like? What title does your business card read? How many people work there? Are you still there? What is the ownership structure?

Delusions of Grandeur Atop Mount Stupid

Ignorance more frequently begets confidence than does knowledge.

—CHARLES DARWIN,
The Descent of Man

The early phases of starting a new company are like the beginning of a new and passionate relationship. The sky is a brighter shade of blue, the air is more crisp. The world is friendlier and more optimistic. I remember the day after I quit my job at IBM to start SimpleRelevance—I ran along the beaches next to Lake Michigan, and I'm not sure if my feet touched the ground the entire way. I was grinning from ear to ear, feeling twenty pounds lighter. My legs were propelled by the sheer enthusiasm of dropping the weight I carried as a corporate drone and riding the wind as a newly-freed soul. My internal monologue rhapsodized about how I would quickly raise my investment round of capital, bring on the talented employees I needed, and conquer the world.

While I like to think I was running toward my exciting new venture rather than running away from my corporate job, I'm pretty sure that elated feeling was a mixture of the two. I worked at IBM for six years. The bureaucracy of those six years was frustrating, but I learned a lot in that time and built an amazing network. The company gave me a lot. And so, while my logical brain knew full well that a voluntary and well-paid career at IBM was the furthest thing from Shawshank Prison, my emotional brain could only sum up the beginning of the entrepreneurial journey with the words of Red Redding from *Shawshank Redemption*, "I find I'm so excited, I can barely sit still or hold a thought in my head. I think it's the excitement only a free man can feel, a free man at the start of a long journey whose conclusion is uncertain."

I was certain I'd be a millionaire at the end of the journey; the only questions were how long it would take and how many times over. Would I take more rounds of venture capital, or would I be able to follow my own destiny quickly, with revenue outpacing expenses as fast as my "conservative" financial models assured me they would? I'm not sure how long I expected it to take until my seedling startup became a full-blown empire, but I certainly wasn't thinking about an eight-year time horizon.

This was the beginning of my Delusions of Grandeur phase.

I love the term Delusions of Grandeur because it reminds me of a particular scene from Star Wars. In *Return of the Jedi*, right after Han Solo is freed from his carbonite prison, he is told by his trusted friend Chewbacca that the bumbling Luke Skywalker is now a Jedi knight and coming to rescue them. Han responds with disbelief, "Luke?…A Jedi knight? I'm out of it for a little while, and everybody gets delusions of grandeur!"

There is a long period at the beginning of the entrepreneurial journey when the only person that may believe you're a Jedi knight of entrepreneurship is the face looking back at you in the mirror. I may have thought I was a Jedi, but everyone else in the world looked at me like a lowly Padawan.[9] They were thinking of me the way Han was thinking about Luke, seeing my inexperience rather than my potential.

That became apparent when I started trying to schedule meetings with VCs, the folks that I blithely assumed would fund me with millions of dollars. Getting them to even take a meeting was *hard*. When I finally got the meetings scheduled, the VCs would oftentimes blow them off, only occasionally with the courtesy of rescheduling. When they did finally show up (usually late), they'd cut the meeting short and spend most of the time on their phones, paying attention to anything but my presentation.

In those moments, in the throes of my Delusions of Grandeur, I was absolutely convinced that I was right, that my pitch was amazing, and that surely these VCs were incompetent. They were arrogant for arriving late and too stupid to understand the brilliance I was bringing to them. Thanks to my overconfidence, I didn't see my own shortcomings, and I misdiagnosed the reasonable doubts of others as arrogance or stupidity.

Looking back, I'm not surprised that people turned me down. There were plenty of flaws with my plan even though I was blind to them at the time. In hindsight, I'm amazed that some kind souls were gracious enough to take me under their wing and say *yes* to invest in me with either their time or money.

---

9   Star Wars lingo for an apprentice.

Remembering these past versions of myself makes me cringe, but I have come to recognize that my mindset was fairly typical for a new entrepreneur. Most of us, at certain stages, have an arrogance born of ignorance and a tendency to disregard any data that doesn't confirm our pre-conceived notions. Entrepreneurs without a touch of that arrogance rarely leave the friendly confines of their day job. Instead, they become "wantrepreneurs" who constantly talk to their friends about the companies they want to create but who never go out and try, the epitome of President Theodore Roosevelt's "cold and timid souls who know neither victory nor defeat."

Dunning-Kruger

Few things in life seem as easy as those which we don't understand. And while philosophers have known that ignorance is bliss since at least the 1700s,[10] scientists have proven this same lack of foresight more recently through a phenomenon known as the Dunning-Kruger effect.[11]

Across a variety of studies, David Dunning and Justin Kruger showed repeatedly that people who are incompetent in a given field are unable to recognize their own incompetence. I was a prime example. Unburdened by the weight of knowledge of what was to come, I was at the height of "Mount Stupid," as they call the peak at the beginning of the curve. In that moment, I saw the inevitable challenges that would come as surmountable (if not easy), and I

---

10   This proverb resembles "What you don't know cannot hurt you." It's based on a passage from "On a Distant Prospect of Eton College," by the eighteenth-century English poet Thomas Gray. https://www.dictionary.com/browse/ignorance-is-bliss.

11   Kruger, J. and Dunning, D. "Unskilled and Unaware of It: How Difficulties in Recognizing One's Own Incompetence Lead to Inflated Self-Assessments." Semantic Scholar. *Journal of Personality and Social Psychology* (1999). https://www.semanticscholar.org/paper/Unskilled-and-unaware-of-it%3A-how-difficulties-in-to-Kruger-Dunning/f2c80eef3585e0569e93ace0b9770cf76c8ebabc.

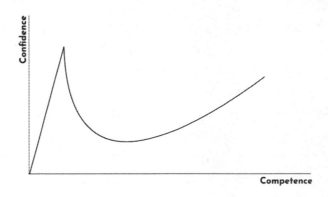

assumed that those entrepreneurs who had tried and failed must have surely been some combination of lazy, stupid, or corrupt. Despite having accomplished very little, this was probably the peak of my confidence.

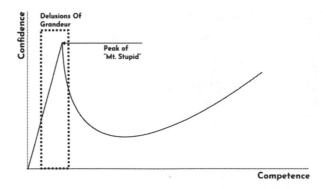

Our internal vision of our accomplishments and potential is disconnected from how others view us—a disconnect that wears down our psyche and causes us to become frustrated and disillusioned. It's maddening when we can't understand why others don't recognize the potential we think is so obvious. And so, we tend to look to external and nefarious forces rather than looking in the mirror. We blame others for their incompetence, stupidity, and bias. We develop all sorts of scapegoats and complain about them to other entrepreneurs who are living the same struggle.

I see this every day with early stage entrepreneurs in the fund-raising conversation. They begin the journey excited, confident, and full of anticipation. Inevitably, they start getting turned down and blame those rejections on some combination of ignorance, arrogance, or prejudice on the part of investors rather than facing the challenging truth that they may need to improve if they hope to succeed in their ambitions.

By the way, I'm not saying that the person on the other end of the meeting is right. I'm not excusing the arrogance of VCs, nor am I suggesting that they aren't sometimes incompetent, stupid, or biased. I can hear many of my readers yelling at me that those biases are real and present challenges that a privileged white guy like me could never possibly understand. And I won't argue with you! Those things may be true, and your righteous indignation may be totally and completely justified!

The scope of this book isn't about systemic change (important as that is); my focus is how to give you the tools to optimize your odds of success (and happiness) given the constraints of the world. Even a privileged white tech-bro like me, with every conceivable advantage, decided that my lack of early success must be about everyone else rather than myself. I grew out my hair and changed my wardrobe, convinced that VCs couldn't take a clean-cut, suit-wearing IBMer seriously as an innovator.

At one point during the countless hours I spent complaining about VCs, someone pointed out to me that "a VC is not your rich uncle." On some level, intellectually, I had always known this. But on some deeper emotional level, I think I assumed that because they *had* money and I *needed* money, it was their job to give me the money that I needed. They are supposed to invest. I'm supposed to build. That's how it works, I reasoned, and if they aren't investing in me, then they obviously aren't doing their part and holding up their end of the bargain!

Later in life, I would come to realize that a VC's job is primarily to fundraise from and manage their Limited Partners—the people who invest in their funds. Their next job is to find reasons to say no to investments. Ninety-nine percent of the time, they are going to say "no." That's just the math of how being a VC works, given how many pitches they get.

I didn't understand this at the time, so I assumed that the reason they couldn't see the overwhelming brilliance of my business plan had to be some sort of deep character flaw that each of them possessed. It was much easier to blame them than to blame myself.

I certainly wasn't willing to admit that my business plan was flawed. In hindsight, it *was* flawed! Most of my assumptions were wrong. Most of the dynamics I predicted were wrong. Before you get too high and mighty, dear reader, your business plan is almost certainly flawed, too. No business plan survives first contact with the cruel world of reality. Go back and look at seed-funding pitch decks for companies like Mint[12] or Uber[13] or some of the others available online. These incredibly successful companies were still wrong in terms of their fundamental business or assumptions.

How your plan is wrong and *why* it's wrong will be interesting lessons to learn on the journey, but that doesn't change the fact that it's wrong. And if you're convinced that your plan is the unique one

---

12   Shah, Hiten. "Mint.com Pre-Launch Pitch Deck." Slideshare.net. January 2, 2010. https://www.slideshare.net/hnshah/mintcom-prelaunch-pitch-deck.

13   Jarvis, Alexander. "Uber Pitch Deck to Raise Seed Capital Investment." 50Folds. https://www.alexanderjarvis.com/uber-pitch-deck-raise-seed-capital-investment/.

that is actually correct, it's a decent sign that you're hanging out somewhere around the top of Mount Stupid. None of that means your company won't be successful. Businesses that succeed and those that fail have a lot in common; to start, they all come from flawed business plans.

But we don't usually have that knowledge when we begin. We don't yet understand the challenges that will take place when our exciting plans encounter the real world. We think we have it all figured out, so the source of the friction, stress, and anxiety in this phase of entrepreneurship comes from the disconnect between your perception of your capabilities and your perception of how others are judging you. Remember that as exciting as this time may be, the data shows that you are most likely standing somewhere near the peak of Mount Stupid. Even if your optimism ends up paying off, at the moment, it's probably not yet justified.

We are going to walk through a number of exercises to help you deal with the effects of the Delusions of Grandeur phase, but for now there are two key things to understand about your perception of how other people are thinking of you:

Number one, they probably are more interested in you than you think. Chances are you are overly defensive and sensitive to any perceived slight. Entrepreneurship is a process of putting your whole self out there and making yourself vulnerable to the core—and it is uncomfortable! I can't tell you how many times someone didn't return a single email, which led me to conclude that this person hates me, doesn't take me seriously, or is generally an asshole. I couldn't get out of my own way long enough to consider the possibility that the other person was just busy and didn't get a chance to respond. Every perceived slight, no matter how small, was magnified in the echo chamber of my defensive and sensitive mind. It took me a long time to recognize this as my ego trying to protect myself from my vulnerability.

But, number two, some people may not actually regard you all that highly...yet! And that *might* be a totally rational response, not one born of stupidity, arrogance, or bias.[14] If you're a first-time entrepreneur, you have a tremendous information advantage over everyone else in evaluating your own potential. You have lived inside yourself forever, and you have likely seen yourself do amazing things and overcome obstacles. You know that you were born for this mission and won't take no for an answer. But you can't blame others for not realizing that fact...yet! They haven't seen it in action. You have to earn their esteem and their capital; you can't assume it will simply be given.

In fact, most people who have been part of the entrepreneurial ecosystem for a while have seen entrepreneurs come and go every year. Over the years, they have spent time with entrepreneurs who don't follow up on their commitments, act with only self-regard, or even lie, cheat, and steal. You may know that you're diligent, selfless, and trustworthy, but how do you convince others? How do you gain their respect so that it matches what you know to be true about yourself?

The only way is to earn it. Every day, through every interaction. The most common side effect of being on top of Mount Stupid is the sense of entitlement that comes with over-confidence. Because you know you're destined to succeed, everyone should be willing to invest time, money, connections, or other resources to help you along the path. Getting past that sense of entitlement and remembering that no one owes you anything is the first step to approaching the help that you do receive with humility and authentic gratitude.

---

14   Again...not saying the bias isn't real or problematic.

We will talk through a variety of techniques to reduce the delusional part of the journey. For now, I'll simply give you the good news that this phase is one that you will almost certainly grow out of naturally. Embracing old-school concepts for a life well-lived is the key to changing how others regard you, day by day. Show up every day, put the work in, follow up, treat others with respect, execute with integrity. As with so many things, it will feel like slow going at first, but you'll be amazed at how quickly you make progress.[15]

By recognizing and dispassionately understanding that we are likely to spend time atop Mount Stupid as we go through the entrepreneurial journey, it will naturally have less control over us. As we go further, we will walk through a variety of exercises and techniques to improve our ability to execute during this phase.

LESSON FROM MOUNT EVEREST

As a person who is constantly jumping into crazy adventures with both feet, I have an endless supply of stories from the top of Mount Stupid. It seems that no matter how many times I go through the cycle, I still find myself in situations where I think I know enough about a topic to be dangerous, but I am actually just dangerously ignorant. One of my favorite examples comes from when my friend, Aaron, first suggested we hike up to the base camp of Mount Everest as an adventure. I thought hiking to Base Camp seemed fun, but naïvely responded, "If we are going to go to Base Camp, why not stick around a few more days and climb the whole thing?"

At the time, I was an avid outdoorsman but had spent most of my time in the Appalachian Mountains (highest peak: 6,683 feet)

---

15 Another similarity between entrepreneurship and mountain climbing. In both, it seems like progress is incredibly slow in the moment. It's only by turning around and looking back that you realize how far you have come.

and had never been higher than the Rockies (14,439 feet). Sure, I had spent lots of time the in the "mountains," but the hills of my experience were tiny compared to the Himalayas. I simply had no concept of the size, scale, and grandeur of the much-higher mountain chain. Ignorance is bliss in allowing you to underestimate the challenges ahead.

I also hadn't read a lot about mountaineering but somewhere along the way had seen that disabled climbers, blind climbers, old climbers, and otherwise impaired climbers had made it to the top of the world. "If they can do it, then a strong, able-bodied young man like me should be able to cruise right to the top," I assumed. As I came to appreciate just how dangerous and difficult the journey is, it magnified my respect for their accomplishments tenfold.

It wasn't that I was dumb; rather that I didn't have any frame of reference for the experience and made some bad assumptions. Thankfully, Aaron was much wiser than me and suggested that I do some reading on Everest before boasting that I could make it up in no time. He was absolutely right.

The hike to Base Camp at 17,750 feet was exhausting, but we made it in reasonably good spirits and health. While catching our breath in the altitude and standing in the shadow of the mountain, I re-affirmed my commitment to climbing to the peak, but with the benefit of a bit more knowledge, I said I would climb it in the next seven years. Even that commitment was naïve—I had no idea what I was truly in for—but it was born of much more knowledge and more respect for the mountain. In the end, it would take another ten years for me to summit, and I was only able to do it and come back down alive with the help of a tremendous amount of both training and good fortune.

TAKEAWAY FOR ENTREPRENEURSHIP

Be conscious of all the things you don't know, particularly when things that are hard for others seem like they should be easy. It may be that you have it all figured out, but more likely you're simply ignorant of the challenges you'll face. That doesn't mean you should fear the journey, but skepticism of one's own knowledge and a realization that you might be somewhere near the top of Mount Stupid will help you calibrate your expectations.

JOURNAL PROMPT

As you consider material assumptions for your business, divide them into three categories: things you know to be true, things you believe to be true, and things that you hope are true. Use this to challenge your assumptions and develop contingency plans.

What hard advice have you heard recently that you have written off as ignorant or prejudiced? In the quiet of your own consciousness, could there be more truth to the advice than you'd like to admit?

What slight from someone else did you chafe at? Is there an underlying sense of entitlement that made that feeling worse?

What percentage do you actually believe it (0–100)? What is the evidence to support it? If the thought were 100 percent true, how awful would it be? Would you survive? Would the people in your life that you care about still love you? What would you tell a friend in this situation?

In five years' time, what do you think you would have to say about this thought? On a scale of one to ten, how helpful or useful is this thought? Is there a different way to think about or approach this thought?

The Death Zone of Imposter Syndrome

One of the painful things about our time is that those who feel certainty are stupid, and those with any imagination and understanding are filled with doubt and indecision.

—BERTRAND RUSSELL,
The Triumph of Stupidity

To reach the top of Mount Everest, or any of the world's tallest peaks, you must spend time at an altitude known as "The Death Zone." It's the altitude above 26,000 feet or about five miles above sea level. At that altitude, the air is so thin that the human body literally isn't getting enough oxygen to stay alive. Muscle tissue breaks down, thinking slows, and the mind becomes cloudy.

I was well aware of The Death Zone's existence when I decided to climb Mount Everest. I knew that my mind and body would be impacted. I knew my physiology and cognition would degrade. I knew it would be challenging and frustrating, but I also knew that there was simply no way to get to the summit without going through the challenge of The Death Zone. That knowledge didn't dissuade me from wanting to climb the mountain; in fact, overcoming The Death Zone was a big part of the allure of the journey. I wanted to see what I was made of, and how I would respond to it. But, knowing it was there, I also made sure to prepare myself.

The Death Zone is an apt metaphor for a certain stage of entrepreneurship. On the way to achieving your goal as an entrepreneur, you will experience periods of high stress and frustration. You'll feel like you don't belong, you'll feel like you aren't thinking clearly, and your body may rebel against you. Preparing for that phase of the journey is critical to your success. Like mountaineering, there's simply no way to achieve your entrepreneurial ambitions without spending time in The Death Zone.

While going through the Delusions of Grandeur phase described in the last chapter is frustrating, what follows is far more dangerous to the entrepreneur.

We spend months or even years toiling away and wishing others would take us seriously in our entrepreneurial ambitions. We want to be thought of and known as entrepreneurs. We want others to see the same greatness in us that we see in ourselves.

Eventually the tides turn, and people start to regard you in a different light. Some of that is just a function of time: as people see you doing something repeatedly, it starts to become more normal and credible. Some of the heightened regard is probably due to your improved ability to explain why your mission is important, how you're going to achieve it, and what it is you're actually building. Some of that improvement may be that your ideas have improved as you have iterated, or you may be getting better at executing.

Eventually, others start to regard you more highly. Investors may *actually* start trusting you with money and funding your company. Employees you have been recruiting may *actually* start to say "yes" and leave perfectly good and stable jobs to help you build your dream. Customers may *actually* start to use your product, some of whom will even like whatever it is that you have created!

This brief moment is the most glorious time of the entrepreneurial journey. The golden moment when everything seems to be in alignment.

It feels like validation of everything you have been working for. The moments when your ego is vindicated! Perhaps your confidence wasn't delusional at all! Others begin to see and validate your vision by investing in your company, signing up to be customers, or coming to work for you. They prove their belief in your vision with their time and money.

This may be the most harmonious phase in the entrepreneur's journey, the brief moment of synchronicity between the entrepreneur and the universe. The entrepreneur feels good about herself, and that confidence is vindicated by some hard-fought and long-overdue wins.

Unfortunately, like so many feelings of harmony and bliss, this one is fleeting, as there are two pressures constantly working to upset the delicate equilibrium. Once again, these challenges are captured by the research of Dunning and Kruger.

The first is a natural reduction in self-confidence. As we learn more about the problems we signed up to solve, the bliss of ignorance melts away, and we are left facing the enormity of the task ahead. The more we know, the dumber we feel! In most humans, this increases our self-doubt and leads to a lower estimation of our abilities. In short, our confidence begins to abandon us even as we are objectively getting better at our job, a phenomenon known as "Imposter Syndrome."

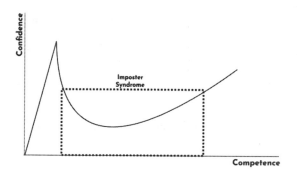

While Imposter Syndrome is a common human experience, there are reasons to believe that this self-doubt is more extreme in entrepreneurs than in the general population. Research shows that entrepreneurs are more prone to a condition called hypomania than control groups.[16] Hypomania is associated with symptoms like unusual amounts of energy, elevated creativity, pursuit of ambitious goals, and propensity for taking risks. As it relates to the Dunning-Kruger framework, hypomanic entrepreneurs are likely to climb higher atop Mount Stupid and then descend further into the world of self-doubt.

At the same time you feel your internal self-regard ebbing, others begin to regard you more highly. Real, actual human beings are signing up to work for you and use your product. They are investing in you. This may start to bring some attention, and coverage from

---

16   Gartner, John D. *The Hypomanic Edge: The Link Between (A Little) Craziness and (A Lot of) Success in America.* New York: Simon & Schuster. 2005.

startup media. At first this feels wonderful; it's the long-sought vindication of all your effort and sacrifice. It proves that your ambition may not have been delusional after all, and other people are beginning to see what you have always seen in yourself!

Alas, following the joy, this dynamic often becomes poisonous for the entrepreneur. The most psychologically dangerous part of the entrepreneurial journey is when we feel like there is more pressure on us to succeed than we can bear. That pressure usually comes from what we think others expect of us. This dynamic of feeling like others expect more than you can live up to is what I call The Death Zone.

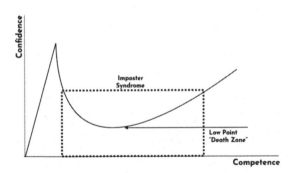

My experience in The Death Zone (and the experience that led me to write this book) was founding and leading SimpleRelevance.

During my most painful time, SimpleRelevance was on the brink of insolvency. We were living on bridge loans as we tried to keep the lights on long enough for some of the contracts customers had verbally committed to be signed and paid. When the loans ran out, I went through the last of my personal savings to make payroll. My parents went deep into their own savings to try to bail us out.

During a very memorable Board meeting, I was all but on my knees, begging the Board for just a little bit more money to keep the lights on and to make a couple more payrolls. Had they said "no" that morning, I would have had to walk out to my team and let them know that day would be our last. Everything would end abruptly and suddenly. I put my odds at about 50/50.

The meeting was a success, and I was able to get the Board to commit a little more money. Precious oxygen to keep operations going for a few more weeks while our receivables could be collected. I wouldn't say I was elated, as I was still under tremendous pressure, but it sure beat the alternative of closing up shop.

That evening, there was an award program for technology start-ups in Chicago. It was a fancy affair with all of the local tech celebrities attending (CEOs, VCs, and the like). We had been nominated for the "Best Business to Business Startup" award.

I can tell you honestly, it never even crossed my mind that we might win that award. Whether it was because part of my psyche still thought I was in middle school and would never be selected by my peers or because of my assumption that somehow the whole community knew our tightly-held secret that we were moments away from shutting down, it just never occurred to me that we might win.

But then, we won.

I got up on the stage, grabbed the trophy, and was back at my table before they could even take a photo. They had to call me back up just for that. Not normally someone who's at a loss for words, I couldn't bring myself to say anything other than a quick and perfunctory "thanks."

Looking back, my reaction makes perfect sense. My mind couldn't process the disconnect. With this award, the entrepreneurial community was telling me that I was the founder and CEO of the best business to business software company in Chicago. When I looked in the mirror, all I could see was a failure that the world just didn't yet recognize. That disconnect made me worse than a failure: it made me a fraud. I was standing in front of my peers accepting an award that felt completely undeserved.

This is The Death Zone.

It's the feeling that you're at the height of others' expectations while being overwhelmed with crippling self-doubt. It's the feeling of Imposter Syndrome that you don't belong. It's the mirror image of the Delusions of Grandeur. Instead of knowing you are meant for something more, but no one else believing in you, this is the feeling that everyone expects you to be able to solve everything, and you simply think you're a fraud.

Elon Musk captured this feeling perfectly in an interview with *The New York Times*:[17]

> "This past year has been the most difficult and painful year of my career," he said. "It was excruciating." Asked if the exhaustion was taking a toll on his physical health, Mr. Musk answered: "It's not been great, actually. I've had friends come by who are really concerned.... It is often a choice of no sleep or Ambien.... If you have anyone who can do a better job, please let me know. They can have the job. Is there someone who can do the job better? They can have the reins right now."

---

17   Gelles, David, Stewart, James B., Silver-Greenberg, Jessica, Kelly, Kate. "Elon Musk Details 'Excruciating' Personal Toll of Tesla Turmoil." *The New York Times*. August 16, 2018. https://www.nytimes.com/2018/08/16/business/elon-musk-interview-tesla.html.

Notice the man that many would consider to be among the most brilliant innovators of all time spoke openly to *The New York Times* about the depths of his despair and his desire to turn over the reins to anyone else who might be able to take over.

To make matters worse, there's one more toxic dynamic that adds to the danger of The Death Zone. We usually come to identify more fully with our role as an entrepreneur even as our confidence erodes.

Most entrepreneurs, when they are starting out, think of themselves as something besides "an entrepreneur" or a "Founder/CEO" of a company. Maybe they are a student working on a startup idea or an employee at IBM with a side hustle. Perhaps they consider themselves first and foremost an athlete or an open-source hacker or an artist or a Cubs fan. Maybe a husband or a daughter or a mother. At any given time in our lives, there are any number of identity groups we may associate with—associations that influence who we consider ourselves to be at our very core.

During the Delusions of Grandeur phase, the annoyance of not being taken seriously is a bit easier to swallow because people don't see you primarily as an entrepreneur. You probably *want* to be seen primarily as an entrepreneur, but at least if you are a "student with a side hustle," you might have a lot of self-regard and confidence by virtue of your academic accomplishments. That makes you feel a little better about not being quite as admired as an entrepreneur. As an undergraduate student at UNC, I always felt like people didn't take me seriously enough as an entrepreneur, but I thought of myself as a pretty good water polo player and open-source programmer.

The Death Zone, remember, is the mirror image. Instead of not being thought of as an entrepreneur, you're probably feeling like the world regards you *too much* as an entrepreneur. By now, you have probably forgotten how to introduce yourself without adding "Founder/CEO of XYZ" attached to it. In fact, you may harbor a sneaking suspicion that the title might even appear on your birth certificate. Your friends and family probably begin most of their conversations with you by asking you about the business. Dates may involve discussions of cap tables or venture rounds.[18] After I sold SimpleRelevance, it took me months to re-learn how to introduce myself without accidentally saying "founder."

If you're like me, for some period of time, you welcome this conflation of your identity with your business. It feels like validation and it feels important—a sign that you have made it! It's not like anyone thinks of Zuckerberg without Facebook or Bezos without Amazon. So being "Erik Severinghaus, Founder/CEO" feels like I'm committed to the business and the world finally recognizes it.

As this repeats itself, our very identity becomes increasingly intertwined with the identity of our company. We don't see ourselves as wonderful parents and successful citizens of our community who just happen to spend a few hours every week on a company we are developing. Eventually, it becomes nearly impossible to view ourselves as separate from our companies. We forget how to say our names without "founder" attached. Like Dr. Frankenstein, our entire existence becomes bound up in the monster that we have created.

This is The Death Zone of Imposter Syndrome. We feel the pressure of others, the doubt within ourselves, and as though our whole identity is tied up in our company. Because this Death Zone

---

18   Not that I'm going to give dating advice…but I don't recommend it.

impairs our judgment and stresses our bodies, it is a dangerous time for both the company and the entrepreneur. It can be exhausting, demotivating, and generally the most miserable part of the journey. It usually comes along with bad decision-making and mistakes that seem hard to believe in retrospect.

It's also nearly universal. Like the world's highest mountains in the Himalayas, the path to the peaks of entrepreneurship usually requires at least some time in The Death Zone. It exists as an obstacle with predictable symptoms and dangers.

The good news is that while The Death Zone is indeed dangerous, its threats can be managed. The symptoms are known and the root causes understood. We will go through them in the next chapters. If you prepare and train for it and approach it with caution and humility, The Death Zone can be managed just like any other obstacle.

LESSON FROM MOUNT EVEREST

There were two people who were incredibly important to my ability to "stay present" daily on my Everest journey. Even though I had previously read a number of books on the importance of that topic, read the stoics during the trip, and constantly reminded myself of the importance of staying in the moment…it was still incredibly easy for me to forget, to look ahead, and to let the scale of the entire journey overtake me.

My first roommate and friend I made on my Everest trip was Mario Cantin, a happy, fun-loving, French-speaking Canadian. We had a bit of a language barrier, which we made up for in the way international travelers do. Lots of smiling, gesturing, pointing, and figuring things out as we went. We ended up being roommates much of the time in tents and tea houses as we made our way up the mountain.

Despite our difficulty communicating, we developed a ritual of celebrating every day as a win. Even on the days that were small hikes or rest days where we did nothing but sit around and play cards, Mario and I would high-five each other and remind one another to celebrate the day. All we had to do was accomplish each distinct day rather than allow ourselves to get frustrated or worry about the entire journey. "One more day," we would repeat to one another. It's probably not a coincidence that Mario made it to the top and back down safely despite being quarantined in his tent for days with pink eye and other infections. Climbing the mountain in honor of his daughter, Melanie, who had tragically passed away at the age of fifteen, Mario was a French-Canadian Zen-master taking the journey day-by-day and grateful for each step.[19]

The other person who kept me present was my good friend and one of the charter members of my support network, Charlie Schmidt. While I had a number of amazing friends from back home sending me encouraging messages that were critical to keeping my spirits up and ultimately my success, Charlie took a slightly different route. Charlie reminded me every day that nothing back home had changed, implicitly helping me combat my fear of missing out on events by assuring me that when I got back, they'd still be there. The Cubs would still be at Wrigley Field, and there would still be a cold beer waiting for me at Murphy's Bleachers. "There is nothing to hurry back to," he would constantly tell me, "so just stay focused on the trip."

---

19   You can read more about Mario's journey at https://ici.radio-canada.ca/premiere/emissions/style-libre/segments/entrevue/74228/mario-cantin-everest.

I have no idea what voice in the universe whispered into Charlie's ear to know the perfect thing to repeat to me over and over, but it was invaluable.

TAKEAWAY FOR ENTREPRENEURSHIP

Find someone to be your "daily celebration" accountability buddy. Who is the person in your life that the two of you can remind each other to celebrate each day of the journey? It can be a journal (a daily gratitude journaling process has a similar effect), but I have found it to be even more powerful when it's someone you know—someone on the journey with you—so you can remind each other, even when it's hard or seems trivial, to celebrate each and every day.

JOURNAL PROMPT

What expectations do you feel like others are putting on you? Are those fair? Do you need to put the expectations of others on your shoulders and carry them through the entire journey?

The Symptoms of Entrepreneurship

Now, when your weapons are dulled, your ardor damped, your strength exhausted and your treasure spent, other chieftains will spring up to take advantage of your extremity. Then no man, however wise, will be able to avert the consequences that must ensue.

—SUN TZU,
The Art of War

The last two chapters discussed the two different types of cognitive disconnect common to entrepreneurship, the frustration in the Delusions of Grandeur phase that people don't expect enough of you, and in the even more toxic Death Zone of Imposter Syndrome phase when you lose your confidence and feel like the world expects more than you can deliver. These are both stressful situations, and going through them can make the world feel out of balance. Research shows that these periods of stress and cognitive disconnect lead to entrepreneurs developing dangerous issues with substance abuse, depression, or worse.

I was no exception.

I have always been an over-achiever. Straight-A student. Salutatorian of my high school class.[20] Eagle Scout. High school newspaper editor. Accepted to the University of North Carolina, awarded a full academic scholarship, and then became captain of the water polo team. I was pretty much always *that guy.* Always seeking praise, constantly determined to be *the best.* It took me a lot of time—and therapy—to realize it, but subconscious striving defined the first thirty-five years of my life.

By the time I started SimpleRelevance, I thought I was an entrepreneurial veteran who knew exactly what it took to compete and win in the startup arena. If you showed me that Dunning-Kruger curve, I would have believed the model but said that it applied to *other* people. I would have been sincere but wrong, thinking I had already visited the top of Mount Stupid, been down through the hard times, and was on the evolving plateau of knowledge. Because I had started more than a dozen businesses since high school (some successes and others failures), I thought I knew what I was getting myself into.

I was very wrong. Those lessons didn't just apply to *others,* and I had to re-learn them the hard way.

I started off, like most entrepreneurs, in my own Delusions of Grandeur phase. Every startup contest I didn't win and every VC who didn't invest made the chip on my shoulder deeper. I cursed the arrogance of the VCs as though I had some God-given right to their money. I chafed against angel investors who were kind enough to give me their time and respected me enough to give me honest feedback on the challenges ahead, hearing only their criticism and not their well-meaning advice.

---

20   Don't even get me started about how I was robbed out of the Valedictorian spot…it still hurts.

Looking back, it's clear that I didn't want to admit that I was feeling vulnerable below the bluster. It's much easier to curse the VC than to acknowledge that they might have a point. Being an entrepreneur is nothing if not a vulnerable experience below the armor, and sometimes, our defense mechanisms make it hard to actually hear the constructive criticism as useful feedback to improve the business...or ourselves. Somewhere inside of me was the kid who wanted the approval of everyone I talked to, unable to admit to others or myself that any response short of glowing praise wounded me.

I was quickly running through the money I had saved from my time at IBM as I paid my team to develop the initial prototype for the business. Enough of the feedback got through my defenses to where I did improve. The business, and my ability to pitch it and inspire others, evolved.

For my first round of capital, I leveraged the only real asset I had at the time—my reputation among friends and family—and raised $110,000 from them. I'll never forget that money, and I'll never forget the people who trusted me enough to back my play. Of all the money you raise as an entrepreneur, the money that comes from the people who trust *you* regardless of your business is the most meaningful. It was a burden I carried through the entire experience, knowing that people trusted me enough to bet on me in such a big way.

After a few more months, we progressed the business to the point that I had a signed term sheet from a respected local VC to raise three hundred thousand dollars. Naïve as I was, I remember two feelings distinctly upon walking out the door with the term sheet signed: I was convinced that term sheet would lead to the money soon being in my account and was further convinced that it was likely to be the last money I would ever need to raise. It seems laughable in hindsight, but I genuinely believed we would quickly scale customer acquisition, achieve profitability, and never need to raise another dollar. Looking back, I was experiencing classic Delusions of Grandeur, overestimating my ability. From high atop Mount Stupid, I thought I had done all the hard work and the rest was going to be easy.

That all came crashing down a few weeks later. I was in New Orleans to celebrate my thirtieth birthday, living the epitome of my "work hard, play hard" ethos (and suffering through the predictable hangover) when I got a call from one of the partners in the venture firm. We were in the finishing stages of turning the term sheet into final documents to be signed, after which they would wire the money. In theory, after a term sheet is signed, the rest of the process is almost perfunctory. In reality, there can be a lot of drama until the money actually reaches your bank account.

"Hi, Erik! Hope everything is going well. I wanted to let you know, we are still excited about investing in the business, but as we finalize the documents, we are going to need to change some of the terms."

My heart sank. "What? We have a signed term sheet. What do you mean 'change some terms?'"

"Well, I have to be honest, man. When I read and agreed to that term sheet, I was at the beach and already had a couple of beers. I didn't read it close enough. I'm sure you understand."

No. I absolutely did not understand.

This moment of heartbreak was so visceral that I can still feel my chest tighten as I write about it eight years later. My entrepreneurial life passed before my eyes.

I left a six-figure job to go be an entrepreneur. I burned through all my savings, raised $110,000 from my friends and family, and now had five people working for me. I leveraged everything I had and realized that the investor on the other end of the phone wasn't going to honor the terms they had agreed to and signed. Even worse, I stopped raising money after the term sheet was signed, so it wasn't like I had another good option. I had no leverage. I could either accept the fact that he wasn't going to honor his signature and renegotiate, or I could take a principled stand in full recognition that I'd probably soon be out of money.

Maybe I should have taken the principled stand and told him to either honor his word or go screw off, but I didn't. We were weeks away from going out of business, and without that capital, I had no idea what I'd do. I couldn't even begin to stomach the thought of losing the money from my friends and family mere months after they had trusted me with it.

And so, the cycle began. The venture treadmill wherein I was always on the verge of running out of money. What I didn't know at that moment was that a few years later, the cycle would nearly break me.

As the pressure grew, so did the symptoms I was experiencing and the toll they would take on me.

I feared I was the wrong person to be running the company, but I was quite sure no one else could or would do it.

I hated going to work, but I hated taking time off even more. Any time not spent working felt lazy and indulgent.

I felt honored that my employees continued to work for me, but I resented any moment they weren't grinding as hard as I was.

I resented them even more for not carrying the same load I was carrying.

I was exhausted but couldn't rest. Stillness scared me more than burnout.

I was terrified of anyone finding out how I felt, even as I wanted to talk about it.

I knew I wasn't living up to the expectations of everyone else, even as I was the one creating those expectations.

For a long time, I soldiered on, burying those feelings—a strategy that worked for years until my body began to betray me. I knew I was stressed out, but I didn't realize I was actually manifesting physical symptoms of the stress until a friend and fellow entrepreneur told me he realized he was at his wits end because his eye had begun to twitch. Wow! That hit me like a ton of bricks. My left eye had also developed a persistent twitch, but I wasn't self-aware enough to realize it might be the result of the stress.

It wasn't just an eye twitch. My tendency to grind my teeth in my sleep got progressively worse, and I began to sleep with a mouth guard. My temper became shorter, and I found myself snapping at friends who showed up ten minutes late to get beers, as though my ego had to remind them of how very important I was.

Those were the symptoms I recognized in myself, but there were plenty more I was blind to. My drinking had picked up a lot, but it was easy to stay in denial about that. I was young and constantly attending networking events that involved booze, surrounded by other high-functioning alcoholics who were also self-medicating. Among that crowd, I felt normal.

I also developed a dysfunctional relationship with my body and exercise. I got hooked on endurance exercise and over-trained to the point of exhaustion. While I remain a huge proponent of exercise as a tool to maintain well-being, I wasn't using it for that. For me, the exercise became a masochistic source of pain and pleasure. It was a way to force myself to continuously run, bike, or swim further and faster. My body tightened up completely, from my neck to my Achilles tendon. I could barely walk or sit, yet I would go out for my daily run, convinced that "when I loosened up, I'd be good for a solid ten miles or so."

Eventually my body fought back. My time in The Death Zone wore me down to the point that I truly feared my body would give out on me. My heart raced, even while sitting on the couch watching TV. My mind began to work against me. Laying in my bed, I caught myself fantasizing about diving head-first off my third-floor balcony. A few moments of falling and my neck would surely snap, ending the pain and misery. I thought about "slipping" in front of the El train as it came into the station. I often thought about the peace that would come if everything would just go dark. The pain of carrying the burden would be over.

Sleeplessness. Depression. Substance abuse. Diet and exercise. I haven't spoken to an entrepreneur yet who doesn't identify with some of these symptoms in their own way and on their own scale. We'll go deeper into each of these symptoms, but if you're having suicidal fantasies like I did, please go talk to someone or call The National Suicide Prevention Lifeline at 1-800-273-8255.

Unfortunately, I know I would not have made that call. Deep in my Death Zone, I wouldn't talk to anyone, partly because I didn't think they would understand, partly because I didn't want to face the shame, and partly because I didn't feel worthy to burden them with my struggles. I would Google search (in incognito mode), trying to learn more about what was happening to my mind and body, trying to understand why I was breaking and how to fix it, but talking to another human was a bridge too far. There was also this persistent shame that I was a comparatively privileged white dude who had brought all of this on himself. My struggle seemed self-inflicted. I didn't feel worthy of help.

I felt like Atlas shouldering the burden of the world, but I would later come to learn that I wasn't unique. In entrepreneurs, these symptoms of prolonged stress are the rule rather than the exception. The symptoms present themselves in different ways but are common to us all. In the next chapter, we will walk through the biology, psychology, physiology and other science behind The Death Zone, and then I will teach you some of the methods I have learned to survive longer and operate more effectively while you are in it. But for now, let's just look at the symptoms to understand what commonly happens to entrepreneurs.

Recognizing the Symptoms

While we are in the pressure grip of the entrepreneurial grind, we usually develop a variety of symptoms. I like to describe the stress as thinking about a balloon: when the air pressure builds up inside the balloon and isn't released, that pressure has to go somewhere. Depending on how you squeeze and shape the balloon, it may go in different directions, and everyone's "balloon shape" is going to be unique, but the physics of the balloon blowing up happens every time.[21]

One of the most dangerous aspects of these symptoms is our tendency to deny them or explain them away. We are masters of deluding ourselves about the fact that these things are actually happening to us. Remember that entrepreneurs have three times the rate of substance abuse and twice the rate of suicidality of the gen-

---

21 I stole this analogy from my friend Jonny Boucher, who runs an organization focused on suicide prevention called Hope For The Day.

eral population. The base case for an entrepreneur is that they will experience some or most of these symptoms, that's just the nature of the journey.

Rather than judging myself for them, I now think about monitoring these symptoms the same way I think about watching my skin for signs of cancer. I know I have a variety of imperfections and moles on my skin; I don't judge their existence or fixate on them. But I do observe them for pain or changes over time. If I notice substantial variation, it probably means something is wrong. In the same way, if I can tell that my behavior or feelings are changing, or people tell me that they are, I try to document and use those anecdotes as data points that merit further examination or maybe even a conversation with an expert.

I stress the importance of *non-judgmental* self-monitoring. While we are in The Death Zone, we already feel like we aren't living up to the expectations of others and don't belong in our position. The primary cause of our stress is the frustration that comes from feeling like we aren't good enough, or that we don't measure up. If we berate ourselves for our mistakes and the bad behaviors we exhibit while under stress, it only makes us feel more unworthy. Those feelings of not measuring up only serve to deepen the shame and reinforce the problems we are trying to solve.

Identify and examine the symptoms. Recognize their existence and manage them as necessary. The symptoms are important and dangerous. But, after this chapter, we are going to focus our energy on the deeper root cause of these symptoms. We will spend the rest of the book learning to identify and work toward solving the root causes, both the physiological causes (stress hormones) and the psychological ones.

Below, I'm going to walk through some of the most common symptoms of The Death Zone and share my experiences and those of others. Your experience is likely to be different (no two people's journeys are the same), but I share this in the hopes that there may be some triggers that allow you to better evaluate your own symptoms. As you're reading about my experiences, what feels true to your experience?

Suicidal Thoughts and Fantasies

I'm going to start with the scariest symptom, suicidal thoughts or fantasies. First things first: this book isn't an authoritative guide to addressing suicide. If you are contemplating suicide, please call The National Suicide Prevention Lifeline at 1-800-273-8255. If that's not your thing, please reach out to a counselor or trusted friend, let them know what's going through your mind, and accept their help. Accepting help is an act of courage, not weakness.

I never did that, and I wish I had. I wasn't willing to let others know what I was carrying. I didn't want to burden them with my mistakes, and it felt *weak* to admit I was struggling to carry the load. I never attempted suicide, but I did have a lot of fantasies go through my mind. I fantasized about the quiet, the end of the anxiety, and the idea of putting down the weight I was carrying. For me, dying felt like a more honorable end to the business than quitting. Putting people through the pain of grieving for me at times seemed easier than facing my failure.

Much like the idea of being in a "prison with the door open," there is a world full of people that are ready, willing, and able to help us carry the burden if we can only be brave enough to put our shame aside, walk out of the prison cell, and have a conversation. It gets easier from there.

It took me a lot of therapy to root out the deep-seated issues that led to these feelings, something I encourage every entrepreneur to consider. I went through the self-evaluation with peer entrepreneurs, professional therapists, and trusted friends.

The one thing I successfully did throughout that dark time was remove temptations to indulge in my suicidal fantasies. I felt my mind working against me, and I didn't want to give it any help in those dark moments. Those fears were a major reason I never kept any firearms in my home or any potentially lethal drugs.

I didn't know it then, but that harm reduction strategy is one of the most effective methods of suicide prevention. Most people who complete suicide go from decision to action in an hour—a majority of those within five to ten minutes.[22] Minimizing temptations for self-harm may have saved my life.

Eating and Exercise

For a while, when people asked me what I did, I thought it was funny to respond that I was a professional masochist. Not in a sexual way, but in a career-choice way. I chose one of the hardest and loneliest professions for myself (entrepreneurship) and then picked hobbies like endurance triathlons and high-altitude mountaineering for my time off. I became addicted to the pain. I loved wearing my body down. I laughed at Ironman training guides and the comparative moderation they suggested, and I worked out far harder. Every minute I wasn't working, I fantasized about running, biking, and swimming. I'd joke I was developing the body of a T-Rex (strong legs, no upper body) and was referred to as "manorexic" by more

---

22 Barber, C. "Means Matter: Duration of Suicidal Crises." Harvard School of Public Health. https://www.hsph.harvard.edu/means-matter/means-matter/duration/.

than a few friends. I assumed they were joking, but looking back, I think they were trying to tell me something.

I loved the discipline it took not to eat the things I wanted. I loved the feeling of superiority I got from looking down on others who didn't put themselves through the pain that I did. I loved the feeling of accomplishing the crazy goals and overcoming the pain to get there. But I wasn't taking care of my body. I wasn't resting or fueling myself properly. In my quest for *more, more, more* I got to the point where my body was so tight, I could barely move. It hurt to walk or stand up, yet I continued to push myself to exercise more.

Sheryl O'Loughlin, the author of *Killing It,* captures this dynamic well in her book. She describes the masochistic tendency toward self-punishment and the reflexive ability to use her intellect to avoid the issue:

> I wasn't thriving; I was slowly killing myself. But the brain works in such complex ways, especially with anorexia, that if you'd told me I wasn't taking care of myself, I would have wholeheartedly argued the opposite. 'Look,' I'd have said, 'despite how crazy things are at work, I'm still taking the time to care for myself by prioritizing exercise. I'm eating fruits, vegetables, and proteins. I'm fine.' Never mind that I'd come to hate running but felt bound to it like it was some twisted, self-imposed prison term.

I still love physical activity, whether it's going to the gym or climbing up a mountain and skiing down. I still want to climb many of the world's tallest peaks. But I have learned to add balance to my routine. I over-train less and balance the weights and cardio with yoga and mobility training. I still try to manage what I eat, but do so from a place of being kind to a body that has done so much for me instead of taking perverse pleasure in self-denial.

Substance Use and Abuse

The National Institute on Alcohol Abuse and Alcoholism (NIAAA) defines more than seven drinks a week for women and fifteen for men to be excessive drinking—guidance that I have always laughed at. Hell, on a good *night* I can put that many away. The federal government thinks that the right amount of pot to smoke is *none*, ever, under any circumstances. I'm not anywhere near qualified to offer a scientific opinion on whether the good people at the NIAAA or the Surgeon General have their thresholds properly calibrated, but I will say that for most of my life, I have been far enough beyond their thresholds to make them irrelevant to my experience and functionally worthless to me.

If you're someone for whom the expert guidance is relevant, fantastic! Please use the expert guidance. I also want to be clear that this book isn't meant to be, nor should it be, a comprehensive perspective on substance abuse or addiction. For those like me who are more likely to laugh at than accept the expert thresholds, I'd like to share one other way to think about the growing frequency of substance usage during your time in The Death Zone.

In my journey, I found that I used substances for two reasons: performance enhancement and self-medication. The performance enhancement piece was the easier one to calibrate and control. I'll get a little bit looser at a networking event if I have a whiskey to reduce my inhibitions. An occasional Adderall can help me get through an all-nighter (or a Board meeting the next morning). This is a dangerous way of thinking because that sort of utilitarian usage can open the door for more extreme abuse, but for many people, a drink to take the edge off isn't a problem.

Where the substances became more problematic for me is not when I was using them intentionally to enhance my performance, but when I was using them to numb my feelings. Research shows that I'm not alone; coping motives are one of the strongest predictors of developing substance-use disorder. In this way, having a drink to be more social was far less problematic than having a drink to numb my feelings about the anxiety of the day. However, it's not as easy as simply saying "don't drink alone," because our minds find ways to trick us on that rule.

One of my best friends from college, Lindsay, and I loved to go out and drink together in the bars around Chapel Hill. Lindsay was a smoker, one of the few vices that I have never really gotten into. Junior year, she decided she was going to give up smoking, but rather than quitting cold turkey, she would wean herself from the habit with a rule that she would only smoke when she was drinking.

You can probably guess what happened next. Lindsay and I went out drinking pretty much every night, she would regularly call me to go have a beer with her just so she could justify the cigarette she was craving. As a good ~~enabler~~ friend, I would naturally oblige.

I never really did a lot of drinking by myself in The Death Zone and would occasionally quit completely for a month or so. It wasn't even tough for me. I wasn't dependent on the alcohol per se, but I sure was abusing it to numb and hide from the anxiety I was feeling. I was self-medicating and using way too much medicine.

Many of you have probably read about the addictive nature of cocaine. A widely-read study showed that rats became so addicted to cocaine that they would request it even at the expense of food.[23] Less widely reported was a 2015 follow-up study where researchers gave mice the same test, but they varied the environment.[24] They found happier mice to be far more resistant to addiction.

This was also replicated in Vietnam veterans who were dependent on opioids while on active duty but were able to readily let go of it upon their return to the comforts of home.[25,26] Addiction is complicated, but there is compelling and growing evidence that environment is a critical component to addiction. When we are in very difficult environments, we are far more likely to seek the comfort of substances to turn off our feelings.

My therapist is fond of reminding me that the brain seeks equilibrium when I ask her about whatever issue I'm confronting at the moment, and substances can present themselves as a tempting shortcut to equilibrium. As entrepreneurs, if we allow ourselves to become miserable in our journey, we are far more prone to addiction. If we allow ourselves to wallow in a cage of our own making, our minds will naturally respond like the mice stuck in their misery

---

23 Perry, Adam N. Westernbroek, Christel, Becker, Jill B. "The Development of a Preference for Cocaine over Food Identifies Individual Rats with Addiction-Like Behaviors." US National Library of Medicine National Institutes of Health. November 18, 2013. https://www.ncbi.nlm.nih.gov/pmc/articles/PMC3832528/.

24 Anwar, Yasmin. "Mice Resist Cocaine If They Have Stuff To Do." Futurity. July 14, 2015. https://www.futurity.org/mice-addiction-cocaine-959182/.

25 Hall, Wayne, Weier, Megan. "Lee Robins' Studies of Heroin Use Among US Vietnam Veterans." *Addiction Classics* Volume 112, Issue 1 (2016): 176-180. https://onlinelibrary.wiley.com/doi/full/10.1111/add.13584.

26 This is not to say that this is the experience of every veteran. In fact, many find returning home to be harder than being with their fellow soldiers in combat. I am only making the point that feelings of stress exacerbate our tendency toward substance abuse or addiction, and feelings of comfort help us resist those urges.

and look for escape, numbing the pain and anxiety through artificial means if necessary. Unfortunately, substances are all too inviting.

Being An Asshole

A friend who is a clinical psychiatrist occasionally reminds me that "depression will often manifest as irritability." I never had the "I can't get out of bed" type of depression, but I sure did manifest my fair share of irritability. Over time, I became more inwardly focused, shorter and sharper in my tone, and less empathetic. I was less caring to my friends and loved ones. I was less forgiving and less flexible.

Friedrich Nietzsche captures the essence of this in his classic quote, "Whoever fights monsters should see to it that in the process he does not become a monster. And if you gaze long enough into an abyss, the abyss will gaze back into you." I fought monsters on a daily basis, but I was slowly morphing into the very type of person I never wanted to be. As I gazed into the abyss of stress and failure, that darkness infiltrated my soul.

Professionally, I always felt like I conducted myself with integrity and humanity. I wish I had taken a little more care in my personal life to similarly prioritize being thoughtful and kind to those around me, especially those who cared for me.

In the next chapter, we will dive deeper into the causes of these symptoms, but suffice it to say, you are highly likely to encounter some combination of them during your journey. Be thoughtful, recognize them, and take care to control how much you let them affect you.

LESSON FROM MOUNT EVEREST

Substance dependence and compulsive exercise aren't the only addictions we can form to escape challenging circumstances. Activity, and particularly digital escapism, commonly shows up as well. Often times it can feel easier to live inside the screens of our phone than in the real world.

One of the most interesting aspects of my Everest experience had nothing to do with the actual climbing, but rather the way my mind responded to being away from screens—what I called "digital detox."

When you're not climbing, you have a surprising amount of free time to read, write, talk, play cards, or engage in any manner of real world activity to pass the time. We had internet access at Base Camp, but it was unreliable and expensive, metered by the amount of data consumed. With typical home internet habits, I could have easily burned through $500 a week.

While I was not really "cut off" from the internet, I used it much less. I probably looked at an electronic device for an average of less than an hour per day. The rest of my time was spent interacting with the real world—talking with humans face-to-face, looking at actual landscapes and objects instead of their digital facsimiles. I read a lot of books, everything from the classics to hilarious sci-fi and fantasy.

I noticed that disconnecting from the virtual world and living in the real world had a tremendous impact on my mind. Even though I try to be kind to my mind by giving it breaks from the digital, I'm still a digital-first millennial who can't remember a time when I wasn't using computers attached to a network. Do you know that feeling where you almost feel naked without your phone? Or that phantom feeling of your phone vibrating or ringing even though it didn't? That weird twitch to look at your phone simply because you haven't checked it in a few minutes, not because you expect there to be anything important on it? All those feelings went away for me over time.

In fact, when I got home, I found myself not wanting to look at my phone or devices at all. I had weaned myself from the dopamine hits of constant stimulation and really didn't want to pick it up. Leaving the sensory-rich, present moment of the physical world for the interruption-driven virtual one felt exhausting. It felt like work, something to be done when necessary, but not a constant desire.

More importantly, I found that I was thinking differently. I had less of a desire to jump from activity to activity. I didn't want to constantly change the TV or radio station. I had regained my ability to think longer thoughts and hold ideas in my head to observe them for longer periods of time. As a result of that, I became less twitchy, less anxious, less irritable, and more grateful. I felt more balanced, more in equilibrium. I found myself less reactive to stressors. I kept thinking "yeah, this may not be perfect…but I can actually breathe the air, and there is living vegetation everywhere!" In contrast to the lifeless and spartan Everest Base Camp, the parks of Chicago felt like the Garden of Eden.

TAKEAWAY FOR ENTREPRENEURSHIP

Entrepreneurship is no less stressful of a journey than mountaineering, and one of the things that makes it even more difficult is that our entrepreneurial decisions must be made while our minds are constantly being interrupted by digital alerts and notifications. The key is to nonjudgmentally monitor these habits, how you're feeling, and how they affect you. Find ways to decompress and slow down, and you'll be amazed how your mood and decision-making improve.

JOURNAL PROMPT

As you read some of the common symptoms of the entrepreneurial journey, which ones do you relate to? Substances? Depression? Do any of them cause a physical reaction in your body?

Knowing it's likely those symptoms will get worse over time, how will you nonjudgmentally monitor those symptoms? How will you be able to tell if you are getting into a warning zone?

Who are the trusted companions on your journey who can help you self-evaluate what symptoms are showing?

The Philosopher and
The Crocodile

My father didn't fly after the war, and he hardly ever talked about it as such, but when he did, I listened. He used to say, "When you walk across the ramp to your airplane, you lose half your IQ." I always wondered what he meant, but instinctively I felt it. When I was a new pilot, I'd get so excited before a flight that I'd get tunnel vision.

—LAURENCE GONZALES,
*Deep Survival: Who Lives, Who Dies, and Why: True
Stories of Miraculous Endurance and Sudden Death*

Ever think you'd fall victim to a con artist? I have always thought that I'm too smart for that. I delete all the emails I get from Nigerian princes asking me for my bank details. I don't give my Social Security number to the fake debt collectors who call me on the phone. I generally consider myself to be a pretty smart guy, and I shake my head in judgmental disbelief when I see other people doing dumb stuff. And yet, as I ventured deep into The Death Zone of Imposter Syndrome, I became the rube. I still have a hard time believing it.

How could I have fallen victim to a con artist? How could I have done such dumb stuff? How did a mind that usually serves me so well come to betray me so deeply? A lot of research and self-reflection helped me to process and understand that what happened to me also happens to many entrepreneurs in similar situations.

Deep in my journey into The Death Zone, I was introduced to a family friend of my then-girlfriend. This relationship was a whirlwind: we quickly fell in love, and she moved in with me weeks after we began dating. I got to know her father who then introduced me to his friend that I'll call "Brad."

I met Brad when he attended a fundraiser I put together for an orphanage in Nepal that was devastated by an earthquake. Brad gave generously to the cause, and we immediately bonded over a shared desire to help others, and to build companies with a leadership mentality that put values first. I thought I had met a kindred spirit, even if he was a bit different.

In fact, from the moment I met Brad, he was an odd character. The former CEO of a publicly traded company and an entrepreneur multiple times over, Brad claimed to be worth tens of millions of dollars and had a cell phone full of rich and powerful names like Arnold Schwarzenegger and Carl Icahn. He was also recovering from a terrible bout with cancer and going through a divorce.

Brad told me that he considered my girlfriend to be a daughter to him through his friendship with her father and that he considered me like a son to him. What's more, he was excited to start fresh, applying his energy, capital, and network to a new entrepreneurial project. He committed to raising a multi-million-dollar round through a combination of personal investment and his various well-connected celebrity friends. Moreover, he would bring in millions of dollars of revenue from his friends who ran various companies around the country. It sounded like the answer to all my prayers.

I had concerns and reservations, but Brad was telling me exactly what I wanted to hear and solving the problems with which I desperately needed help. I checked him out with a few references and he seemed to be legitimate. Because of our personal connection and relationship, I overlooked some of the warning signs and repeatedly gave him the benefit of the doubt; I assumed his good faith and integrity in a way that I would come to regret.

What sorts of "warning signs" did I miss? I'm glad you asked. Buckle up.

As a result of his cancer, Brad was in tremendous pain. When he was in the office, it was hard to tell if he was intoxicated, high, or simply trying to medicate for his discomfort. He would routinely miss meetings, supposedly for medical reasons. A disruptive force in the office in the best of times, he was a constant distraction for the rest of the team and for me. At one point, I had to tell him to stop bringing handguns into the office. Another evening, he seemed confused, wandering the halls and talking to himself.

As the bizarre behavior escalated, Brad disappeared for a few days. When he resurfaced, we found out that he crashed his car while driving it just a few blocks and was taken to jail after the cops discovered he was drunk with a car full of firearms.

I know this sounds crazy but bear with me. It doesn't just keep going—it gets worse.

He was a volatile and emotional person, and while he was kind of a weird old man, he was *my* weird old man. He got upset if I had outside fundraising conversations, swearing up and down that our fundraising problems were over thanks to his capital and connections. As I became frustrated with more talk and no action, we sat down with the company's lawyer and drafted a term sheet that documented his commitment to immediately invest one million dollars personally. This happened in parallel with him bringing in a signed contract from a local, well-known hospital for $7 million.

Bowing to his pressure, I shut down all my fundraising discussions, leaving me dependent solely upon his money. He showed me signed documents—worth millions of dollars—that would generate momentum and get us to the critical mass we so desperately needed. As the bizarre behavior escalated, my dependence on him did as well.

My intuition screamed at me not to trust him, but his background did check out, and I needed him to deliver on his promises. As Upton Sinclair famously remarked, "It is difficult to get a man to understand something when his salary depends upon his not understanding it." More than my salary, my entire existence as an entrepreneur increasingly depended on Brad coming through on his commitments.

Although he delivered signed term sheets and contracts, cash never quite seemed to reach our account. As the excuses mounted, I grew increasingly desperate. We had exhausted our cash, our lines of credit, and we were running on fumes. Actually, we were beyond fumes; I was pouring my savings in to the business to make payroll every two weeks. He had incredible stories about his difficulty getting the money out of various off-shore financial havens in Caribbean islands (where he was allegedly sheltering it from his allegedly cheating ex-wife), but he was effusive that the money was coming "tomorrow or the next day." I felt like I was dying of dehydration and always being told that I'd get a glass of water "tomorrow."

Over Labor Day, my girlfriend and I planned to take a quick, three-day backpacking trip in Denali National Forest. Since I had yet to receive the money Brad had promised, I called him to tell him I was going to cancel the trip. I didn't feel like I could miss a half-day in the office.

I'll never forget the conversation, Brad's voice telling me that my worries were nonsense. "Erik—your money problems are over. There will be a million dollars in the company account when you get back on Tuesday, and tens of millions more coming in shortly thereafter. Go, relax, have a good time, and get ready to scale this company when you get back. Do you really think I'm going to let you and my 'daughter' down?"

So off we went. Of course, the money wasn't there when I got back; instead I had to dig deeper into my personal savings to cover yet another overdraft of our corporate account and have yet another miserable conversation with our bankers. Later that week, he sent me a text with what was supposedly a wire confirmation of the million dollars being internationally routed from his account to mine.

When I sent the confirmation to my banker, he responded that the confirmation was invalid; in fact, it didn't even have the correct number of digits.

As he told me that, I physically lost my breath. The charade in front of my eyes came crashing down, and I realized the money was never going to come. The signed contract with the hospital was similarly fraudulent, and my worst fears were realized. Informing the Board was one of the hardest things I have ever done; this was the end of the road, and I had to find some sort of an exit as quickly as I possibly could. One day, I was telling the Board we had a million dollars of funding coming in, and that we were booking millions more in revenue. The next day, all of that disappeared, and we were on the brink of collapse. Although it happened suddenly, somewhere in the back of my mind, I had known it was coming for weeks.

In hindsight, it's blindingly obvious that I missed the forest for the trees. I had intellectually identified the various risks that ended up sinking us, but they were too hard for me to process, and I avoided honestly confronting them for too long. My vision was too narrow. My energy was too depleted. My mental state was too compromised.

So how did I get there? I'm not a dumb guy, how did I make such dumb decisions? Why did my brain delude itself into trusting Brad?

How Our Brains Work Against Us

The human mind is the most complex and wondrous work of nature we have ever discovered. It does so many things incredibly well, like controlling our body, keeping us breathing, eating, and communicating. It allows us to create art, theorize about the beginnings of our world, discover the most basic building blocks of physics, and be aware of our very selves in ways that no other organism yet discovered is.

So why, given the amazing sophistication of our minds, do they go haywire on the entrepreneurial journey? Why do the stresses of entrepreneurship cause us to exhibit all of the depressing and even dangerous symptoms we discussed in the last chapter? And how could such a wonderful instrument let me down when it came to Brad?

Our miraculous minds are, unfortunately, poorly calibrated for modern-day challenges. All of the sophisticated machinery of the mind honed by millennia of evolution is really designed to do one single thing exceptionally well—create the conditions that allow us to survive long enough to reproduce and pass our genes on to the next generation. In some ways, our bodies are simply vessels for our DNA, and the mind is the organ that takes information in and regulates the outflow of energy to allow us to reproduce our genes. Our minds and bodies are finely tuned to work in harmony for that purpose.

Surviving long enough to reproduce is no small feat, especially over the hundreds of previous generations during which our ancestors were constantly beset by danger. One day, we might have needed to escape from a bear; the next day, we might have needed to fight a rival to the death if we wanted the opportunity to mate and reproduce. For most of our history, our ancestors had to be constantly aware of how we were perceived by our tribe; if we were cast out from our social circle, it likely meant death. Individual humans didn't survive long in the wild and certainly had a much lower probability of reproducing.

Our minds and bodies evolved in harmony to meet these demands. We developed hormones like adrenaline and cortisol to give our bodies an extra boost if we needed to fight or flee. We developed a complex understanding of our social dynamics and a paranoia about maintaining our social status. Humans of previous generations who weren't sufficiently paranoid or quickly triggered to action were much less likely to survive, reproduce, and pass down their DNA.

We are all the product of our most violent and paranoid ancestors.

These instincts and physiological tics are critical if you are trying to outrun a predator or outfight a rival. Unfortunately, these same chemicals and adaptations that keep us alive under extreme physical duress have side effects that also wear us down and make us far less effective in our current environments. They are great for fighting bears, but not so great for building enlightened companies over the long term.

The mind is constantly on the lookout for dangerous situations, a paranoia that's required for survival. Unfortunately, our minds are not sufficiently evolved to separate the danger of "holy shit, a bear is about to eat me" from the danger of "my lead investor in my seed round is pulling his support for my Series A, which creates a signaling risk and increases the odds that I'll get stuck in the Series A crunch." From your mind's perspective, that financial risk might as well be a giant bear you're staring at, and it triggers the responses that have worked so well for generations who need to be ready for a bear fight.

Here's what happens inside your body when you sense danger. Your mind signals your body to produce and dump two chemicals, cortisol and adrenaline, into the bloodstream. The effect is like spraying nitrous oxide onto an engine. They prime you to move faster and to work harder than you are designed to do, in short bursts.

- Your heart rate increases, pumping blood through the body to be ready to fight or flee.
- Your vision narrows, allowing you to avoid distractions and focus on the danger at hand.
- Your digestion stops, maximizing energy available in short bursts.
- Your IQ plummets as blood in your brain flows away from the cerebral cortex (where complex reasoning is processed) to the amygdala (where reactions occur).

- Anxiety increases, pushing you to action through a general feeling that you must not remain in this uncomfortable situation.

- Empathy drops, preparing you to do horrible things to others (historically that included literally killing them) to ensure your own survival.

- You excrete alarm pheromones to make sure that others around you know that you are in danger.

The speed of that reaction is no accident. Our minds are designed to short-circuit the thinking process in dangerous scenarios, to act on instinct and without thinking since the time it takes to process the thoughts might get us killed. This is a dramatic oversimplification,[27] but you can think of the brain as having evolved three major systems over time:

- The Jellyfish: The brain stem is the core motor system, the interface that connects our brain to our body. This is, in an evolutionary sense, not all that different than a jellyfish. Very primitive, it's the mechanism that sends electrical signals telling our muscles to contract or relax, our heart to keep beating, and our lungs to take in air.

- The Crocodile: The limbic system is the core emotional system. It wraps around the brain stem and contains primal emotions, pleasure, pain, and sensory responses. In an

---

27 When I say, "dramatic oversimplification," I mean it. Complex subsystems make up the brain, and lots of fascinating studies exist on how the brain works. I'm collapsing complexity into what I think is the most fundamentally important takeaway: our brains are not homogenous, they contain different parts, and those different parts react to the same stimulus in different ways. That disconnect feels weird until we become comfortable with it. Readers with a background in neurobiology will notice that I have taken some liberties in my simplification. If you're interested in reading more about the inner workings of our minds, I'd suggest *Mind: A Journey To The Heart of Being Human* by Daniel J. Siegel or *Buddha's Brain: The Practical Neuroscience of Happiness, Love, and Wisdom* by Rick Hanson and Richard Mendius.

evolutionary sense, it's akin to the sophistication of a crocodile.[28] It tells us to be angry or lustful, and it rewards the rest of our brain with happy chemicals like dopamine when we follow its instinct.

- The Philosopher: The cerebral cortex is the reasoning and logic system. Its sophistication is uniquely human. You can think of it as a renaissance philosopher weighing the cosmic pros and cons of actions you might take, analyzing their impact on others or the environment and trying to make you into the best version of yourself.

All of these are well-adapted and almost miraculous responses to danger. They help keep us alive and improve our odds of reproducing. But what works wonders when confronted with a hungry bear is the wrong response to the Series A investor scenario.

Studies have shown time and again that humans respond in predictable ways to making decisions under pressure.[29] Our vision narrows, our attention shrinks, and we adopt simpler modes for processing information. During your time of greatest duress, when you need to be sharpest and most able to process information, all those abilities go out the window. When the typical entrepreneur encounters the stress of a business conflict, they have less ability to

---

28 Technically, many of the emotions referenced are actually mammalian, not reptilian. They are probably a bit too complex for a crocodile. The metaphor that's often used is the idea of an elephant and a rider, originally described by Buddha in The Dhammapada. I'm using the crocodile as a slightly different metaphor; it represents the part of us focused on survival and procreation über alles with no regard or empathy for others. The philosopher is focused on the higher good. It's not a perfect metaphor to map the crocodile to the limbic system and the philosopher to the cerebral cortex, but exploring the deeper complexities is out of the scope of this book (and there's plenty of great literature on these ideas already).

29 Kowalski, Kathleen M., Vaught, Charles. "Judgment and Decision-Making Under Stress: An Overview for Emergency Managers—CDC." https://www.cdc.gov/niosh/mining/UserFiles/works/pdfs/jadmus.pdf.

process information, think clearly, relate to others, and maintain their moral compass.

Even worse, while you are trying to "fake it 'til you make it" and convince your investors and employees that everything is under control, your body is literally betraying you by sending off olfactory alarm bells, letting everyone know that something isn't right. An important nuance to remember is that this isn't about being "cool" or "strong" or "tough." There's no judgment to this. This is simply human physiology. Hormones. Chemicals. It's just the way our bodies work as a result of hundreds of generations of evolutionary tuning.

Unfortunately, our bodies don't betray us only in the moment; chronic exposure to stress means things get worse over time. The sleeplessness, indigestion, and cardiovascular issues compound. We develop irregular heartbeats, high blood pressure, potentially even heart attacks or strokes (otherwise healthy entrepreneurs have suffered both in their twenties). We develop tics, like the eye twitch I mentioned. Chronic stress exacerbates anxiety and depression as well as suicidality. Neither the body nor the mind is equipped to handle these chemicals being dumped into the bloodstream day after day, so we develop various symptoms in response to this distress.

And so, as the VC threatens you with pulling the term sheet, your brain and body sense the danger, prepare you for battle, and *shut down* the mental processes that might actually help you solve the problem. You see less sharply, think less clearly, become more agitated, and generally are less effective at every dimension of analysis and persuasion when faced with a complex problem.

Even worse, with all the chemicals being dumped into your bloodstream, you may feel the euphoria of rising to the occasion! Among those chemicals is dopamine, the pleasure drug. In a cruel twist of irony, the evolutionary maladaptations to modern-day threats trick us into thinking they are valuable even as they reduce the discernment and judgment we need most.

All of this is our brain's limbic system, the Crocodile brain, trying to save our bodies from danger so that we improve our odds of surviving to reproduce.

If you're like me, it becomes even more frustrating because your cerebral, Philosopher brain feels the blood pressure rising and tries to intervene. "Calm down," I tell myself, "keep cool." I imagine the dialogue between my Crocodile brain and my Philosopher brain as something like this:

Croc: Philosopher! You're in danger! I'm going to put the body on red alert until you solve this problem.

Philosopher: No...stand down...everything is fine. We have food, water, shelter, and physical safety. No need for red alert.

Croc: So now you're calling me stupid? I've kept these genes alive for millennia by "overreacting"—no way I'm listening to you.

Philosopher: This red alert is only making me angrier, sleep less, prone to drink more, and think less. It's doing more harm than good!

The argument continues. For me, this cognitive dissonance only increased my frustration and shame. My Philosopher brain understood I was a privileged white guy who quit a six-figure job to go on a journey of my own choosing. My Philosopher brain knew my survival needs were well taken care of and had this notion of a truly "cool" Gary Cooper-type entrepreneur who didn't feel the stresses I was going through. Because I saw these natural responses as weaknesses, they fed my self-loathing and shame.

My mental disconnect also put stress on my body. It made me more irritable and less able to sleep. Lacking more effective tools to mentally reconcile the Philosopher and Crocodile, I resorted to crude ones like booze and pot to shut them both up. That disconnect between the limbic system and the cerebral cortex was the single biggest cause of stress for me during my journey.

Eventually, I developed better tools. When I finally learned to listen to the Crocodile, acknowledge him, appreciate him, and then use him, that dissonance went away. I may not always appreciate the evolutionary adaptations that make my life more difficult. I wish my armpits didn't perspire when I am frustrated or excited. I wish my blood pressure didn't spike when I sense a relatively trivial threat in a work context. But rather than discounting and ignoring these subsystems of my body, I now thank them for keeping my ancestors alive so that I might be on this planet and have learned to interrogate these signals and symptoms so that I can reach an internal harmony.

How does all of this explain how I became the rube in Brad's bizarre con?

Like many entrepreneurs, I'm a natural optimist with a positive outlook. I tend to think the best of people. I saw the world as I wanted it to be, rather than for what it was. Somewhere deep in my gut, I knew something wasn't right, but I didn't have the courage to interrogate that suspicion. In this case, my Crocodile knew something was wrong, but I was too exhausted and burnt out to listen. I was too desperate for the fantasy of help that Brad was peddling.

I suffered from confirmation bias, putting more weight on the evidence that confirmed my hopes, rather than the evidence that contradicted them. Amid the most stress I have ever gone through, I confused a con artist and an addict for the answer to all my business pressures. It seemed too good to be true and turned out to be a complete lie.

As I've reflected upon the experience, I have tried not to let myself become jaded by Brad or any of the other instances where trusted mentors have betrayed me. I think my positive outlook and mentality of abundance do far more good than harm in my life, and I would rather not give in to the temptation to become more paranoid and defensive. On the other hand, I no longer question whether there are bad actors in the world. As optimistic entrepreneurs, we can be particularly easy prey for liars and those who look to take advantage of us. Recognizing that, I am much quicker to set and enforce boundaries, limiting contact or trust in those who show themselves to lack ethics or integrity. When my Crocodile is telling me that something isn't right with someone, I have become much quicker to listen and take action to protect myself and others.

One of the biggest surprises I encountered when researching this book was how many entrepreneurs have experience with their own "Brad."[30] I thought I was the only one who could have been dumb enough to fall for this sort of a con, but I was wrong. Amid the entrepreneurial journey, otherwise intelligent and independent people become particularly susceptible to a certain type of savior persona. Trusting Brad was far from the only bad decision I made as an entrepreneur, but it was one I had the hardest time understanding until recently.

In the next chapter, we will examine the ways that bad advice in the community reinforces our propensity to make bad decisions under stress. From there, we will examine a variety of specific strategies to become more resilient and less likely to make mistakes like trusting the wrong people.

---

30   Carman, Ashley. "This Backpack Has It All: Kevlar, Batteries, and a Federal Investigation." The Verge. March 4, 2020. https://www.theverge.com/2020/3/4/21156136/iback-pack-smart-backpack-kickstarter-indiegogo-crowdfunding-scam-investigation-ftc-doug-monahan.

LESSON FROM MOUNT EVEREST

One of the calling cards of the Crocodile brain is the tendency to perceive danger and create discomfort in your body until you respond, and this can happen in strange ways. Some of the hardest days on Everest were rest days. It seemed like rest days were the days people quit the most often. It wasn't the climb that sent most people away; it was the quiet contemplation in the tent that led people to throw in the towel.

Not all rest days were created equal. Some were well-deserved, expected, and fun. A day off after a tough day's climb might be nice. But at the end of the day, I wasn't there to rest. I was there to climb. Climb harder, climb faster, climb higher. Achieve. Act. Win. Conquer. This is the lingo of the hard-charging mountaineer!

Except that it's all bullshit. One of the most important things my guides did was force me to slow down. Take the acclimatization hikes slower. Take more days off. Rest my body more. There was a constant focus on having the energy and focus ready for when we needed it, not burning it all up in pointless activities.

I didn't take particularly well to that philosophy at first. The first few times I asked our lead guide to go do more work, hike higher, and push harder, he patiently explained that what my body needed was more rest and acclimatization, not further stress. Eventually, he just rolled his eyes when he saw me coming. When I was feeling good, I wanted to show off. I wanted to *do stuff*—not rest. And especially not rest for multiple days in a row!

Perhaps the worst were the unplanned rest days. Bouts of weather that would strand us for more than a week tested all manner of patience. Some of those rest days were more exhausting and frustrating than the tough days of climbing.

But accomplishing great things like climbing to the top of the world requires tremendous amounts of rest and time for recovery. Looking back, if I had been in charge, I would have wanted to climb Everest faster, more aggressively, with only nominal rest between the hard days. I would have paid lip service to the idea of recovery but found excuses to constantly push for more and more activity.

Thankfully I had guides who impressed upon me the importance of rest and recovery. Otherwise, there's no way I would have had the energy I needed to make it up and back down safely in the condition I was in. Had I burned my energy on pointless displays of activity earlier in the trip, I wouldn't have had what I needed when it mattered.

TAKEAWAY FOR ENTREPRENEURSHIP

Understanding how our minds work is key to performance. When we can harmonize the various competing voices in our minds, we are more likely to perform well and less likely to make terrible mistakes like trusting the Brads that come along. Prioritize rest and recovery if you want to have the strength to execute with energy and focus when you need it most.

JOURNAL PROMPT

Reflect on a dumb decision that you made in the heat of a stressful situation. How did your body feel in that moment? How did your mind feel? What emotions existed? How can you use pattern recognition to identify if you're in a similar situation and put in circuit breakers?

Exposing the Broken Entrepreneurial Advice Industry

If you have the rewards, you must also get some of the risks, not let others pay the price for your mistakes. If you inflict risk on others, and they are harmed, you need to pay some price for it… If you give an opinion, and someone follows it, you are morally obligated to be, yourself, exposed to its consequences.

—NASSIM NICHOLAS TALEB,
Skin in the Game

One of the most frustrating parts of being an entrepreneur is the sheer number of people that want to give you advice, and how bad most of that advice is. In fact, studies show that the more entrepreneurial advice you listen to, the less successful you are likely to be!

Imagine running a corporate division coming up for review. In this review, 75 percent of your employees failed to meet their performance goals and either quit or were fired. Your employees had three times the rate of addiction and twice the rate of suicide as the rest of the company. And, while a few of your employees were incredibly successful, over the past eighteen years, your division returned a rate of return (IRR[31]) of 6.6 percent, while your peer divisions were between 8 and 11 percent. How would you rate this division?

The inescapable conclusion would be that things are fundamentally wrong. The process to recruit and train employees, and to operate the business, must be broken. No one in their right mind would call the combination of financial underperformance and heartbreaking outcomes for employees anything other than a debacle. If you ran this division, you would rightly expect to be fired.

And yet, these numbers essentially sum up the state of entrepreneurship right now in the United States. There are a variety of different statistics depending on the time horizons and vintages of companies that one uses as well as how we define "failure"—but most credible analysis shows about 75 percent of companies that have been venture funded don't return meaningful capital to their equity investors.

If the data shows that the environment is littered with high potential companies that died, we might think that surely investors are making enough money on the successes to justify the cost of all these failures. Once again, the answer is no. Once you adjust for

---

31 While by no means the only measure of success, Internal Rate of Return (IRR) is one of the most important metrics for investors to understand whether their investment is a better use of their capital than their alternatives. The more risk involved in an investment, the greater the IRR needed to justify that risk.

fees, risk, and the lack of liquidity in venture capital, the returns[32] very rarely justify the asset class.

According to the 1Q 2018 PitchBook Benchmarks,[33] the internal rate of return (IRR) for the VC industry was 6.6 percent between 2Q 1999 and 2Q 2017. Over those eighteen years, the VC IRR was lapped by other forms of private equity (10.5 percent), debt financing (10.1 percent), and fund-of-funds investing (8.1 percent), despite the fact that most of those investment classes have lower risk and greater liquidity.[34] Limited Partners would be better off investing in an S&P 500 index fund than in the median venture fund.

It's not just investors who are saddled with poor outcomes; entrepreneurs are similarly suffering.

Dr. Michael Freeman penned a wakeup call to the industry in his pivotal research, *Are Entrepreneurs "Touched with Fire"?*.

Who in their right mind would choose to be an entrepreneur? The barriers to success are virtually unlimited and most startups fail as a result. Entrepreneurs have lower initial earnings, lower earnings growth, lower long-term earnings, greater work stress, and more psychosomatic health problems than employees.

So, why do the entrepreneurial and VC industries continue to exist? In fact, there's an entire cottage industry of researchers writing papers that explore the cognitive delusions that mislead people into

---

32 Swedroe, Larry. "Exposed: The Myth of Private Equity and Venture Capital Outperformance." Advisor Perspectives. July 6, 2016. https://www.advisorperspec tives.com/articles/2016/07/06/exposed-the-myth-of-private-equity-and-venture-capital-outperformance.

33 "PitchBook Benchmarks (as of 2Q 2017)" PitchBook. 2018. https://pitchbook.com/news/reports/1q-2018-pitchbook-benchmarks.

34 Liquidity is the ability to put more money in or get your money out whenever you want.

taking the entrepreneurial journey.[35] Many of these academics spend lots of time trying to find the "nonpecuniary" benefits that cause us to throw our lives away tilting at windmills. They are usually at least a bit condescending in their academic language like Daniel Kahneman when he writes in *Thinking, Fast and Slow*: "More often than not, risk takers underestimate the odds they face, and do not invest sufficient effort to find out what the odds are. Because they misread the risks, optimistic entrepreneurs often believe they are prudent, even when they are not."

The moral I take from the statistics above is that the average entrepreneur, following our current entrepreneurial system, is likely to fail. The very definition of a broken system! But while others wonder why anyone would decide to be an entrepreneur, I have an almost religious conviction that entrepreneurship is critical for both society and for those of us who feel called to become entrepreneurs. My takeaway from these statistics isn't "don't be an entrepreneur," but rather, "don't pollute your brain with the advice that is causing an entire industry to fail."

I'm going to avoid the rabbit hole of "why be an entrepreneur" for the moment and simply say that I believe it's the same reason that other creators create. Most artists who feel called and driven to create do so to satisfy their souls, not based on a rational cost benefit analysis of the available options. The best answer mountaineers can

---

35   These are three of my favorites, but there are plenty more: Åstebro, Thomas, Thompson, Peter, "Entrepreneurs, Jacks of All trades or Hobos?" *Research Policy*, Volume 40, Issue 5 (2011): 637-649. https://www.sciencedirect.com/science/article/abs/pii/S0048733311000199.

Astebro, Thomas, Herz, Holger, Nanda, Ramana, Weber, Roberto A., "Seeking the Roots of Entrepreneurship: Insights from Behavioral Economics" *Journal of Economic Perspectives*, Volume 28, Issue 3 (2014): 49-70. https://www.aeaweb.org/articles?id=10.1257/jep.28.3.49.

Spivack, April J., McKelvie, Alexander, Haynie, J. Michael, "Habitual Entrepreneurs: Possible Cases of Entrepreneurship Addiction?" *Journal of Business Venturing*, Volume 29, Issue 5 (2014): 651-667. https://www.sciencedirect.com/science/article/abs/pii/S0883902613001080 ?via%3Dihub.

come up with for climbing to high places is "because it's there." I think the academic focus on the outcome misreads the value of the journey itself.

The inescapable conclusion is that the whole model is broken, and I believe it starts from the fact that we don't teach entrepreneurs the right lessons. If everyone is listening to the same advice, and most are failing, maybe it's time to re-think that advice. What has become obvious to me is that the entrepreneurial ecosystem has evolved to take advantage of the natural optimism of entrepreneurs, goading them into all sorts of excessively risky behavior—the opposite of resilience.

Consider research published in *The Journal of Small Business Management* in 2017. Richard Hunt and Kip Kiefer found that the "Entrepreneurship Industry (EI)"[36] is a $13 billion market segment growing at 12 percent annually, which makes it one of the fastest growing industry segments in the world. Unfortunately, they also showed that entrepreneurs who consume *more* of the services provided by this industry are *more* likely to fail. The *more* books, movies, and conferences on entrepreneurship you allow to pollute your brain, the less likely you are to succeed!

Another study, this one by Rasmus Koss Hartmann et al., takes the attack by academia on entrepreneurship one step further. In "Towards an Untrepreneurial Economy?" they suggest the entrepreneurial economy is in decline because unserious people don't want to call themselves "unemployed." Thanks to the low barriers to entry, it's much sexier to refer to oneself as an "entrepreneur" than a "bum." I have often heard these and other aspiring entre-

---

36   What they call the Entrepreneurship Industry, I'm going to call the Entrepreneurial Advice Industry (EAI). I think my nomenclature is a bit more precise, but we are basically talking about the same thing.

preneurs called "wantrepreneurs," but Hartmann is even more dismissive and calls them "Veblenian Entrepreneurs," named after Thorstein Veblen, whose book in 1899 invented the idea of "conspicuous consumption." The idea behind the paper is basically that many unserious people call themselves entrepreneurs to sound cool to their parents or on their Tinder profiles, thus bringing down the whole industry. Hartmann thinks that the Entrepreneurial Advice Industry essentially manufactures these entrepreneurial "muppets," like a factory cranking out bad widgets.

While these papers are important studies for their rigor, like so many academic studies on entrepreneurship, they miss the "why" and "so what" parts of the question. The Entrepreneurial Advice Industry exists, as do entrepreneurs some would identify as "unserious." But the $13 billion industry that is built to develop them doesn't seem to be helping, and in fact may actively be doing harm to the community. Unfortunately, it's the entrepreneurs that pay the cost of this advice and are left by the wayside when they go broke or end up completely broken.

However, I don't think it's a satisfying response to these papers to suggest that entrepreneurs stop soliciting advice as they navigate a new and uncertain journey. There is lots of value in learning from the lessons of others. Having been deeply ingrained in the Entrepreneurial Advice Industry for essentially my entire life, here's where I think it goes wrong and how you can participate while preparing your brain to call BS on the bad advice.

The Danger of Volatility

To understand why the Entrepreneurial Advice Industry is so broken, you need to understand volatility. Starting a business is an inherently risky and volatile endeavor, both for the business and for the founder personally. But, as you go through the journey, you'll have to make choices that will either increase or reduce that volatility.

There's no magic formula to determine how much risk to take on, or how much volatility to embrace. Fortune favors the bold, after all. But remember, all the research shows that it takes about eight years for the entrepreneurial journey to pay off. It's important to be cautious and thoughtful about taking risks that reduce your odds of making it to that eight-year horizon.

The entrepreneur usually has only one bet to make…her company. She may get to make multiple bets by being a serial entrepreneur, but at any given point in time, her personal financial wellbeing is largely dependent on just one thing—her company's value.

Being cautious about increased volatility is about more than just financial outcomes. From a psychological perspective, the human mind values stability over volatility. As we discussed in previous chapters, the stress of volatility is hard on our physiology. Our minds and bodies view volatility as risk and danger and ramp up our stress hormones accordingly.

And so, for financial and physiological reasons, volatility makes resilience much more difficult. While there are certainly times for bold action and volatility-inducing bets, entrepreneurs are generally better off when they are able to reduce volatility and increase predictability.

The rest of the industry, on the other hand, craves volatility. Their entire business models are built on it. As we deconstruct the Entrepreneurial Advice Industry, this lens of volatility will be very important.

The Three Filters of Entrepreneurial Advice

If you're an entrepreneur listening to advice on how to be more effective, you are almost certainly getting it through one the following three filters. If, as the evidence shows, the Entrepreneurial Advice Industry is failing entrepreneurs, we have to look at these three gatekeepers to understand why.

While entrepreneurs should be thinking about managing, and oftentimes, reducing volatility to increase resilience, each of these filters of entrepreneurial advice have reasons to be in the "pro-volatility" camp. By luck or design, each of them have profited from volatility, and by the time they are successful enough to be invited to give advice, they probably have little to lose from it:

- Investors (VCs and bankers) who invest in companies
- Reporters who write about the entrepreneurial world
- Successful entrepreneurs who have had exceptional exits

These givers of advice are usually insulated from the most important risk the entrepreneur faces – the risk of ruin should the company fail.

Let's go through each of these three filters to understand their conflicts.

Why Investors Love Volatility

VCs look to make outsized returns on capital invested from the hard work and creativity of the entrepreneur. They make more money when the entrepreneur succeeds, a fact they will usually repeat ad nauseum to show that they have skin in the game. They are less likely to mention all the ways that they hedge their downside risk.

They take their management fees, usually 2 percent of invested capital, regardless of how their investments perform. They also structure elaborate preferences in their financing documents, limiting their downside risk if the company doesn't do as well as expected.[37] But the most important difference in the dynamic between entrepreneurs and VCs is that VCs have a portfolio of investments rather than a single bet. They don't really care whether *your* company succeeds or fails, so long as *some* of their companies succeed wildly. They need volatility for each of their companies so that some of them will generate the outsized returns. The idea behind this is that if there is enough volatility in each portfolio company, some of them will win big and generate huge returns.

Of course, in a perfect world, all companies will be volatile in a positive direction, growing, scaling, and generating outsized returns. VCs rightly recognize this as a pipe dream. However, if the investor can drive each company to make bigger bets and be more volatile, they have a better chance of creating some big wins. Their entire model is driving volatility, writing off the losers, and reaping the rewards from the wins. Remember, "the losers" make up 75 percent of the average VC portfolio. They expect to write off three of every four investments. They expect three out of every four entrepreneurs to lose everything they have put into their business.

The VC investment model reminds me of gamblers at a track wagering on racehorses. They cash big checks on the long-shot winners, but the losing horses are put out to pasture or shot dead on the

---

37   Seriously, make sure you understand the preferences of any fundraising round
      you put together. Preferences, interest payments, dividends, and other fine print
      are oftentimes more important than valuation. *Venture Deals: Be Smarter Than
      Your Lawyer and Venture Capitalist* by Brad Feld and Jason Mendelson is the best
      primer I have found on the esoteric but critical elements of fundraising.

racetrack when injured. Being left lonely and abandoned is the most likely outcome for the typical entrepreneur.

Why Reporters Love Volatility

It's not only VCs who crave volatility. Reporters monetize the entrepreneurial ecosystem by generating page clicks reporting on successes, but they also generate huge traffic for stories of failure. What they really want is action! Interesting stories of dramatic change, either growth or collapse. What they crave, in a word, is volatility. They don't want boring, typical stories, and they are often all too happy to take cheap shots at an entrepreneur to sensationalize the narrative and drive traffic.[38]

Why Successful Entrepreneurs Love Volatility

This is a classic example of survivorship bias in action.[39] Entrepreneurs who were successful enough in their outcomes to speak are by definition the outliers. They are the 25 percent who succeeded through some combination of luck, skill, and perseverance. They are the exceptions to the rule, the ones for whom an outsized risk paid off, despite the odds.

38　A tragic example of how cheap shot reporting can contribute to the entrepreneurial crisis and a compelling retrospective can be found in the story of Austen Heinz: https://www.inc.com/jeff-bercovici/austen-heinz.html.

39　Survivorship bias: "the logical error of concentrating on the people or things that made it past some selection process and overlooking those that did not, typically because of their lack of visibility. This can lead to false conclusions in several different ways. It is a form of selection bias.

Survivorship bias can lead to overly optimistic beliefs because failures are ignored, such as when companies that no longer exist are excluded from analyses of financial performance. It can also lead to the false belief that the successes in a group have some special property, rather than just coincidence (correlation proves causality). For example, if three of the five students with the best college grades went to the same high school, that can lead one to believe that the high school must offer an excellent education. This could be true, but the question cannot be answered without looking at the grades of all the other students from that high school, not just the ones who 'survived' the top-five selection process."

Survivorship bias—Wikipedia. https://en.wikipedia.org/wiki/Survivorship_bias.

Creating a Brainwashing Echo Chamber

Imagine that you're selected to be the head of the $13 billion Entrepreneurial Advice Industry and want to brainwash a group of entrepreneurs into taking massive risks that may or may not be in their best interest. How do you convince them to put their mind under the constant strain of volatility when it might be worse for their finances and will certainly be more dangerous to their psychology? You're trying to convince them to gamble mightily, despite a 75 percent chance of failure. How would you do that?

If it were me, I'd construct a propaganda echo chamber. Within that echo chamber, I'd select the 25 percent of entrepreneurs who had previously been successful and create examples out of them, exalting them to almost mythical status as deities to be worshipped and emulated. I would create fawning documentaries and TV shows to reinforce their fame. The 75 percent of entrepreneurs who fail would be totally ignored or, if they were discussed at all, I'd find ways to blame their lack of financial success on personal failings. They were weak. They didn't fight hard enough. They weren't all that smart or committed. It's never the model that failed, it's always the entrepreneur. The implication would be that those who win are the ones who possess the virtues of a hero, and those who fail are contemptible failures of a human being. By personalizing success or failure, I have a better chance of convincing entrepreneurs to ignore their own self-interest and risk mitigation.

I would take full advantage of the tendency of the human mind to absorb stories and ignore data. Force-feeding my subjects a steady diet of successful anecdotes and the occasional autopsy of failure that identifies and emphasizes the personal failings of the entrepreneur, I'd convince them that their success is preordained. Ms.

Entrepreneur, I would constantly implore, don't you see yourself as one of those 25 percent who are successful? Surely you don't identify with the 75 percent who are losers…right? Failure is for the weak, I would remind them, ignoring the inconvenient fact that most companies fail.

I'd trumpet ideas like "do more faster" and the need to "go all in" on every panel, speaking gig, and media appearance. If I'm a VC, I'd remind them that there is some alignment in our outcomes (VCs do make more money when entrepreneurs do well), but I would surely forget to mention that I have a hedged portfolio to protect me from the downside of any single failure. I'd tell stories of all those successful entrepreneurs who took on great risk and, through daring and cunning, became wealthy beyond all imagination. I'd tell them to keep betting big because "failing is part of succeeding." Entrepreneurs who didn't take on the risk? Those lazy "lifestyle entrepreneurs" just didn't have the guts to play with the big boys. I wouldn't just question their wisdom; I would imply that they are cowards.

But, I'd also know that for all my stories and brainwashing, the most compelling speakers wouldn't be the VCs and bankers; they would be fellow entrepreneurs. Getting them to tell their stories would be key. They would be candid, earnest, and speaking authentically. They would tell entrepreneurs their truth in the most honest way they could. And so, I would select which entrepreneurs and stories to amplify.

The lie wouldn't be in anything these entrepreneurs say but in selection bias of only hearing from the most successful. The only ones selected to speak would be the small percentage for whom constantly taking on more risk actually paid off. The few who injected outsized volatility into their company, and had it work!

Is any of this sounding familiar? This hypothetical echo chamber almost perfectly describes our real-life, toxic Entrepreneurial Advice Industry. The $13 billion industry that is failing our entrepreneurs, a self-perpetuating ecosystem of players serving their own self-interest by encouraging as much volatility in the entrepreneurial world as possible.

It sure fooled me. Like many entrepreneurs, I pride myself on thinking differently than others and going my own way. I hate to admit it, but I was completely fooled by this echo chamber. I bought into all of this bad advice.

Every one of those volatility-inspiring talks and articles only reinforces one of the two poisonous dynamics we talked about earlier: the Delusions of Grandeur chip on your shoulder or The Death Zone of Imposter Syndrome.

Let's say you're struggling in your fundraising and chafing in the Delusions phase, frustrated that the world won't take you seriously as an entrepreneur. Seeing that another company just raised $20 million only deepens that chip on your shoulder, reinforcing the perception that you're being unfairly victimized by a world that doesn't give you an honest opportunity because of any one of a number of unfair dynamics. If you're living through the Imposter Syndrome phase, that same news article only reinforces the idea that you aren't good enough because someone else figured it out, and you haven't been able to. Either way, polluting our brains with all this news only makes our minds less effective.

Ask yourself, if a VC has 75 percent of their portfolio fail and an average IRR that lags the S&P 500, what gives them the right to sit on a panel and tell you how to run your business? Why on earth would you listen to them? As Nassim Nicholas Taleb writes in *The*

Black Swan: The Impact of the Highly Improbable, "The graveyard of failed persons will be full of people who shared the following traits: courage, risk taking, optimism, et cetera. Just like the population of millionaires. There may be some differences in skills, but what truly separates the two is for the most part a single factor: luck. Plain luck."

There are four particularly common and dangerous categories of bad advice that are perpetuated by the Entrepreneurial Advice Industry:

The Answer to Everything is More Activity
Classic Example: "Do More, Faster"

The bad lesson I took from this: Rest, thought, and introspection are just different words for "analysis paralysis." To achieve, always seek more activity.

"Do more, faster" was something I heard a lot during Techstars, a highly selective accelerator program I went through with SimpleRelevance. I got to know David Cohen and Brad Feld, two of the founders of the program who are highly respected (for good reason) leaders in the entrepreneurial community. Their core value as an organization is "give first," and in my experience, the entire leadership team of Techstars has their hearts in the right place; they have done more to help entrepreneurs than almost any organization out there. Brad, in particular, has written bravely about mental health in startups and the need to de-stigmatize issues like depression.[40]

But even organizations with the best intentions and great results can perpetuate dangerous behavior. Techstars taught me to play the

---

40   Feld, Brad. "Bringing Depression Out of The Shadows In Startups." FeldThoughts. April 8, 2015. https://feld.com/archives/2015/04/bringing-depression-shadows-startups.html.

entrepreneurial game very well, but I never stopped to ask myself whether I should be playing it at all. I certainly never considered what effect that game would have on me as a founder.

During the last month of Techstars, we focused all of our time and energy on creating, refining, and mastering a ten-minute pitch that we would give to a room of investors from around the country on stage at the House of Blues in Chicago. It was the closest I would ever be to becoming a rock star. The idea behind this event is to flip the traditional supply and demand paradigm by assembling all of these investors in one place with a limited number of companies, so the VCs clamor to invest in the presenting businesses.

The pressure of the whole program, and particularly that last month, is intense. Each of us went through more than one hundred iterations of our presentation. Creating, pitching, refining. Throwing the whole damn thing away and then starting over. Rinse, repeat. All with that Demo Day date staring you down, unchanging. Just when I thought I perfected the message and the pitch, a brilliant and successful mentor would listen to the pitch and utterly eviscerate it with feedback like (correctly) calling it "the most boring ten minutes of my life." And so, I would start over again.

What comes out of this concentration of intellect and effort is an incredible work product. I learned more about crafting a narrative, creating a compelling presentation, and delivering it with style in that month than I ever thought possible. The exercise was wildly effective for the dimension it focused on; it transformed my pitch and created fundraising interest. I'm eternally grateful to Techstars and the leaders of my cohort[41] for everything I learned through the process.

---

41   Thank you, Troy Henikoff, Steve Farsht, and Sam Yagan.

The side effect is that by the end of the process, everyone is completely mentally fried. More than half of our cohort of ten CEOs ended up crying at one point or another during this month. Everyone's emotions were on overdrive as we fueled continual effort on a cocktail of adrenaline, anxiety, and whatever amphetamines happened to be floating around.

By the end of the program, I could tell I was at the end of my rope, so I planned to take a vacation over the final weekend before Demo Day to visit a friend at his lake house. The idea was to spend some time enjoying nature, recharge my internal batteries, and get ready for the coming event.

My well-meaning mentors hated this idea; it went against the entire ethos of "do more, faster." All the other companies were staying and working through the weekend. Everyone was going to be busting their asses refining their pitches and practicing. What kind of a lazy bum disappears to go water skiing and swimming for a weekend when there's such a big event on the horizon? Commitment was proven by working harder and doing more, faster! More activity, dammit! There will be time for rest after the program.

I let myself get talked out of the trip. I was bummed, but there was no sacrifice I wasn't willing to make for the company, and I certainly wasn't going to put my presentation at risk.

At Demo Day, it seemed my decision to skip the relaxation was vindicated. My presentation rocked. We were in the coveted final spot—the anchor position—and I nailed it. All the hard work, long hours, and emotional turmoil paid off. I truly felt like a rock star as I came off the stage getting high-fives from everyone.

I soon got caught up in even more activity, and I never did take that weekend to relax after the program. Looking back at the swirl of action, activity, and arrogance, it's clear in hindsight that my priorities were all wrong. The successful pitch generated investor interest, but in my arrogance, I didn't take advantage and raise money. I reasoned that the company's upward trajectory was unstoppable, and I decided to optimize on the variable of "preserving equity so I would get a better percentage at exit" rather than "raising capital to increase our resilience and chances of surviving." Big mistake.

The program and advice of Techstars delivered exactly as advertised and got me to the point I wanted to be. They did their job, but I was idiotic to the point of entrepreneurial malpractice to not raise a large amount of capital when there was so much excitement around the business. Techstars taught me how to be a better entrepreneur, but I missed the boat on realizing that the most important thing was to put myself in a position to survive as long as possible. I wasn't optimizing for an eight-year journey.

I don't know if a weekend at a lake house would have given me the rest I needed to zoom out and get better perspective. But the mantra of "do more, faster" removes the nuance that activity needs to be balanced with perspective. Yes, entrepreneurs need to stretch the limits of their energy to execute. Yes, entrepreneurs often need to be snapped out of their analysis paralysis. No doubt, they often need to understand that "perfect" can be the enemy of "good" and they simply need to make decisions and move on. There's also the realization that entrepreneurship is really hard work requiring herculean feats of mental strength and stamina in even the best situations.

But there are times that entrepreneurs also need to do less, slower. Think. Manage emotions. Find the easier or better solutions. Resist the temptation to use activity to avoid contemplation.

Your Worth as a Human is Determined by the Outcome of Your Company
Classic Example: "The Struggle"

> The Struggle is not failure, but it causes failure. Especially if you are weak. Always if you are weak.
>
> Most people are not strong enough. Every great entrepreneur from Steve Jobs to Mark Zuckerberg went through The Struggle, and struggle they did, so you are not alone. But that does not mean that you will make it. You may not make it. That is why it is The Struggle.
>
> —Ben Horowitz, "The Struggle"[42]

The bad lesson I took from this: Business failure is caused by personal weakness. I am only as strong as my company's income statement. If I were strong enough, we would be succeeding. Since we are not, I must be weak.

Ben Horowitz has written one of the definitive ruminations on The Death Zone. In "The Struggle," he captures many of the psychological and physiological effects, the self-loathing, the anxiety, even the digestive issues. Any entrepreneur can relate to his words, and I read them repeatedly while I was in The Death Zone. Horowitz does an admirable job of capturing what it's like in poignant and poetic prose.[43] I have never met Horowitz, but I believe that he means well in trying to empathize with and help entrepre-

---

42 Horowitz, Ben. "The Struggle." Andreessen Horowitz. https://a16z.com/2012/06/15/the-struggle/.

43 Mark Suster has another good rumination on the true life of the entrepreneur in his post about what he calls "Entrepreneurshit." https://bothsidesofthetable.com/entrepreneurshit-the-blog-post-on-what-it-s-really-like-67963eaa1119.

erik z. severinghaus

neurs (he even donates the proceeds of his book to helping women going through "The Struggle").[44]

But the takeaway from "The Struggle" only reinforces the bad advice of the Entrepreneurial Advice Industry. It's counterproductive to entrepreneurs and (perhaps unintentionally) only reinforces the VC notion that the answer to problems lies in increased volatility.

Horowitz doesn't really define what "failure" means in this essay, but if I could find one recurring theme in his book, *The Hard Thing about Hard Things*, it's that a sufficiently determined and intelligent entrepreneur can always find a way through whatever challenges arise in the course of starting and growing their business. I don't think I'm uncharitable to equate Horowitz's notion of failure with shutting down a company.

The corollary he constructs is that the weak never make it through The Struggle, and most people are weak. The strong can always find a way, whereas the weak are doomed to fail. In other words, if your company must shut down for some reason, it is your fault as an entrepreneur for your contemptible weakness.

In my experience, the only thing this advice does is make it harder to forgive yourself, live in the present, and execute. When I was knee deep in The Struggle, I hated myself for it. I hated myself because I wasn't succeeding. I hated myself even more for every minute I didn't work, any time I spent not trying to succeed. I thought of myself as weak. Reading "The Struggle" was a form of catharsis for me, but also subtly reinforced my self-loathing.

---

44   Horowitz, Ben. "Why I Will Give 100% of My Book Earnings to Women in the Struggle." Andreessen Horowitz. https://a16z.com/2014/02/25/why-i-will-give-100-of-my-book-earnings-to-women-in-the-struggle-2/.

No one has a crystal ball to understand who will succeed and who will fail while building companies. I have seen plenty of amazing, hardworking, courageous entrepreneurs who ended up closing down or taking an acquihire.[45] I have seen plenty of entrepreneurs I respect a lot less go on to be unbelievably successful. There are lots of variables that impact entrepreneurial success, and luck may be the most important one. Equating success with strength is meaningless on its face and does nothing to help entrepreneurs.

Go All In
Classic Example: Chris Gardner—*The Pursuit of Happyness*

The bad lesson I took from this: Ignore the voice in my head that is uncomfortable with volatility. Instead, take on more risk, because that's what you do if you believe in yourself, and it's bound to pay off in the end.

Let's take, as a popular example, the true story of Chris Gardner as depicted in the popular film *The Pursuit of Happyness.* It's one of my favorite entrepreneurial stories, the amazing tale of a man who believes in himself, takes extreme risks, loses everything, but through hard work and grit, eventually emerges successful as a rich and famous titan of the financial services industry. The most gut-wrenching scene of the movie is when Chris, utterly penniless, misses the curfew for the homeless shelter where he's staying with his son. In complete desperation, he's forced to huddle in a disgust-

---

45 "Acquihire" (acquisition + hire) is entrepreneurial lingo for an acquisition that really only results in the employees getting a job at the acquiring company. It basically means that the company got bought but investors don't make money. There is usually a nice press release where "terms of the acquisition are not disclosed," employees get to keep their jobs, and the product usually continues to exist and serve customers. Unfortunately, the investors usually get little to no capital returned in this scenario.

ing public bathroom in the subway, barricading the door to try to protect himself and his little boy from intruders and danger.

The story has the typical narrative for entrepreneurial literature, and we celebrate Chris for his grit and determination. In retrospect, his success appears almost pre-ordained, as though Lady Fortuna[46] was always going to ensure that Chris would win the single-coveted spot at his trading firm and go on to fame and fortune. In that context, from the position of retrospectively inevitable success, Chris seems heroic for leaving his job for the unlikely opportunity to make something more of himself. The doubters in his life, especially his contemptible wife who leaves him when she can no longer handle the volatility, are clearly cowards.

Let's consider the completely plausible scenario where Chris does everything right and should have won his position, but a racist hiring manager decides to give it to a white guy. Or a scenario where someone else wins, despite Chris's hard work, due to a family connection Chris lacks. In that parallel universe, you might say Chris would have just found another way due to his talent and unrelenting grit. But each time he did this, he took substantial chances with his family's safety. What if he had been overrun by a gang or senselessly killed by a lunatic in the bathroom that night?

The point here is that, while we can celebrate the grit and determination of folks like Chris Gardner, we need to put it in the context that they are the exceptions. They are so exceptional and unusual that they inspire a bestselling book and then movie to tell their story. Chris is not only amazingly strong, he also gets quite lucky.

And remember, Chris isn't just gambling with his discretionary money; he is rolling the dice with his son's physical safety. We

---

46   The goddess of luck and fate. Fortuna—Wikipedia. https://en.wikipedia.org/wiki/Fortuna.

can surely agree that there must be some point where risk-taking becomes unjustifiable, even immoral, regardless of the outcome. We may celebrate the entrepreneur who takes out a second mortgage on the house or risks the kids' college fund and succeeds, but there also has to be some point where the sacrifice and risk to herself and her family goes too far. Some point where the entrepreneur's *unwillingness* to ask more of others or even herself becomes not the weak course of action, but rather the strong one. The smart one. The right one.[47]

You are already taking tremendous risk and daring greatly through the very act of believing in yourself to be an entrepreneur. Equating *courage* with constantly increasing your leverage and risk serves only the volatility-seeking parasite class feeding on the entrepreneurs. Remember that volatility is great for them but toxic for you.

Focus on the Exit
Classic Example: Shark Tank

Whether I flip on *Shark Tank* or sit on an entrepreneurial panel, there is always some discussion about how much money to raise at the "low" valuations early in the journey. The focus of this conversation is dilution and how much that percentage of the company will be worth at exit. It usually takes some form of "if you take $1 million at a $10 million valuation, you are giving away 10 percent of

---

47   In the final days of SimpleRelevance I was becoming increasingly resigned to the fact that we wouldn't be able to make it. The friends and family who were the first to invest, and in many ways had the most to lose, kept offering to dig deeper to keep us afloat. Eventually, even though it hurt me to my soul, I had to refuse their overly generous offers to invest more. Looking back, I'm still proud I made that call.

the company.[48] If you take $2 million, you are giving away 20 percent. If you sell for $100 million, that's the difference between you taking home $80 million and $90 million!" Often, even the articles that say "don't focus on dilution" make the case in terms of final economics at the exit. Either way, the entire discussion is framed in the future (economics at exit) instead of the present (optimizing joy on the journey and odds of success).

The bad lesson I took from this: As an analytical person, I took these kinds of mathematical models to heart and built all kinds of excel models to analyze my personal outcomes, given various financing rounds at different prices and terms. As a closeted masochist predisposed to take on as much pain as possible in the near term to optimize eventual gain, I was all for this tradeoff! I avoided available capital as a matter of principle, showing how tough and what an efficient operator I was. I made my journey harder and more volatile while trying to mathematically optimize my future payoff.

Now, to be clear, there are also risks associated with taking more financing. You should make sure to have trusted attorneys and conduct due diligence on your investors.[49] There are many stories of entrepreneurs being taken advantage of in early rounds of financing only to regret it later—so I'm not suggesting not to be thoughtful in how you raise early stage capital.

But there is a subtext to the advice of avoiding capital and dilution now for the promise of a greater eventual payoff. It can become a badge of honor, enduring whatever it takes now to optimize returns later. That message is absolute madness. It's that sort

---

48 Nitpicking readers: yes, I know this isn't technically true; I'm keeping the math easy (but directionally correct) for the example.

49 The best way to find a trusted attorney for startup fundraising is to ask other entrepreneurs in your ecosystem who they recommend. Don't use general purpose lawyers or family friends for something this important.

of influence along with my bad judgment that led to me not raising money when it was available.[50] My friend and amazing investor, Mark Tebbe, puts it even more succinctly when he tells his students to "fill up your plate while the buffet is open."

If I had optimized raising capital around "how to build the best company possible" and "how to enjoy the journey being resilient to the ups and downs," I would have been much more thoughtful (and focused) on raising the money I needed to survive challenges and downturns. Instead of focusing on the present state of my company, I focused on future hypothetical returns. This was a huge mistake that left me undercapitalized.

Given the selection bias and conflicts of interest, is it any wonder that the Entrepreneurial Advice Industry is failing in its mission so dramatically? It's a shame and results in tragic financial and human consequences.

The rest of this book is my answer to how we can better prepare entrepreneurs for the road ahead. By focusing on the entrepreneur and helping them develop mental resilience to be successful on the journey, we can help them be better prepared for what is to come.

LESSON FROM MOUNT EVEREST

For as long as humanity has had language, we have used stories to pass down wisdom to future generations. Those stories are incredibly powerful; novices listen to the stories their elders tell and pattern their behavior accordingly.[51]

---

50 There is also an element of stubbornness that can take hold. In the early stages, I felt like I couldn't get anyone to invest. Later, when capital was available, some part of me didn't want to take that money out of sheer pique.
51 My favorite exploration of this topic is a series of interviews collected as *Joseph Campbell and The Power of Myth with Bill Moyers.*

If we tell stories celebrating risk, it will inspire those that come next to take on more risk, which can end tragically. The mountaineering community has come to understand the importance of the stories we tell, the impact they have on our listeners' behaviors and the risks that they take. There's this general sense that mountaineers are devil-may-care risk takers, constantly putting themselves in harm's way for the glory of standing atop a high point. If you watch mountaineering movies made for the general public, they'll reinforce the notion that risk is something to be glorified in the pursuit of a great adventure.

Most of the books you'll read by mountaineers, in contrast, couldn't be more different. Yes, there are daring feats contained in the pages, but they constantly discuss mitigating risk rather than taking more of it on.

Ed Viesturs is the first and only American to have climbed all fourteen of the world's highest mountains, and for good measure did so without using supplemental oxygen.[52] He is probably the most respected American mountaineer alive. His most famous philosophy focuses on risk mitigation "getting to the top is optional, getting back down is mandatory."[53]

When I reached the top of Everest, that phrase kept repeating itself in my mind. Getting down is mandatory. I still needed to get back down safely.

In fact, modern mountaineering is full of protocols, safety checks, and a general safety-first mentality. This isn't an accident. As

---

[52] The most exclusive club in mountaineering is made up of the people who have climbed the "14 eight-thousanders" which is a short way of saying the mountains on earth that are above 8,000 meters, or about 26,000 feet high.

[53] His fantastic memoir *No Shortcuts to the Top* repeats this mantra over and over again, including a story where he turned around a mere 300 feet from the summit of Mount Everest to make sure he could get back down safely.

a community, we have learned the hard way that ignoring the inherent risks of the sport leads to horrific outcomes, including death. Jon Krakauer chronicles how risk-taking can end tragically in his book *Into Thin Air*, which vividly depicts the deadly results of arrogance in dangerous situations. The difference is that almost anyone who writes stories about mountaineering is probably a mountaineer him or herself. They know just how dangerous bad advice can be. The keepers of mountaineering lore have far more skin in the game.

Entrepreneurship, unfortunately, has had no such reckoning. Our mythology, the stories we pass down to the next generation of entrepreneurs, are usually about piling risk on and persevering through those situations. We celebrate stories like Fred Smith winning the money to save FedEx at the blackjack table or Chris Gardner spending the night with his son in a public bathroom.[54]

In contrast to the caution I was taught by mountaineering mentors, every entrepreneurial story I heard was about taking on more and more risk. I have undergraduate and MBA degrees focused on entrepreneurship, have been through two accelerator programs, and have heard more entrepreneurs speak than I'll ever be able to count. Not one of them, that I can remember, ever suggested that entrepreneurs be thoughtful about how they take on risks or advised them to take care of themselves first.

TAKEAWAY FOR ENTREPRENEURSHIP

Entrepreneurial stories, lessons, and lore would do well to learn from those of mountaineering. Celebrating daring accomplish-

---

54   Zhang, Maggie. "The Founder Of FedEx Saved The Company From Bankruptcy With His Blackjack Winnings." *Business Insider*. July 16, 2014. https://www.businessinsider.com/fedex-saved-from-bankruptcy-with-blackjack-winnings-2014-7.

ments without an honest acknowledgement of the risks involved is not only dishonest, it invites disaster from copycats and imitators who may not be as lucky. The data is clear that we as an entrepreneurial community are a struggling and vulnerable population, and it's past time that we help new entrepreneurs understand and honestly reckon with what they are in for.

JOURNAL PROMPT

Think of the last couple of entrepreneurial speakers you have heard give advice. How much of that advice seemed geared toward making them look tough, wise, hardworking, or important on the stage? How often did those talks earnestly delve into their failings or where they could have done better?

The Resilience Cycle

They're called the Eight Worldly Winds: pleasure and pain, praise and blame, gain and loss, fame and ill repute. As you develop greater equanimity, these winds have less effect on your mind. Your happiness becomes increasingly unconditional, not based on catching a good breeze instead of a bad one.

—Rick Hanson,
Buddha's Brain

Now that we have laid bare the challenges of the entrepreneurial journey, it's time get into solutions. Throughout the rest of the book, we will go through a series of time-honored, scientifically proven methods for building resilience.

The road of the entrepreneur is different for everyone, but the toll that it takes on those of us who walk down the path is fairly predictable. It's a hard road made more difficult by the fact that our physiologies as humans are poorly adapted to these particular stressors, and the fact that most of the advice given to us that's supposed to be helpful actually makes things worse.

The bad news about our natural human psychology and physiology is that we are designed to react poorly to the stresses of entrepreneurship. The good news is that, because these types of stresses are universal to the human journey but simply more acute in entrepreneurs, they have been studied extensively by researchers and philosophers alike who have found ways to equip us for these challenges.

As we discussed in previous chapters, you won't find useful solutions in the entrepreneurial literature we so often read. In reading the usual suspects, you'll be inundated with bad advice like "do more, faster," "the strong survive, so don't be weak," and perhaps my favorite answer to every question, "hustle harder." Sometimes I wonder if all entrepreneurial advice gets channeled through Ron Swanson[55] and is thus designed to make the speaker sound tough without any regard for what actually works. In fact, following most of that advice results in more volatility, making survival less likely. The opposite of resilience.

Resilience is all about how to survive and keep going despite the challenges. Some of the best advice on resilience comes from the direst of human circumstances, surviving in dangerous and life-threatening situations. Despite vastly different times, places, and challenges, survivors tend to have much more in common than you might think; research has shown a certain consistency to the survivor's mentality.[56] By adapting that mentality, we can make ourselves more resilient and improve our odds of succeeding through the entrepreneurial gauntlet.

---

55   If you have somehow missed out on the glorious machismo of this iconic *Parks and Rec* character, the following link will give a you a sense of his essence: https://www.msn.com/en-us/travel/news/inspiring-quotes-by-ron-swanson-of-parks-and-recreation/vp-AADzgNr.
56   Siebert, Al. "The Genesis of the Survivor Personality." Al Siebert Resiliency Center. https://resiliencycenter.com/exceptional-mental-health/.

Default Alive Versus Default Dead

There are many parallels between entrepreneurship and survival research. Paul Graham, a noted startup luminary and founder of YCombinator, understands the importance of the fight for survival in the startup world. He developed the insight that one of the best ways to classify companies is along the dimension of "default alive" or "default dead."[57] Most companies we think about in the world are "default alive." These are companies like IBM or GE that generate revenue and profits. If their revenue and expenses continue at their current trajectory, these companies will continue to make payroll and exist for the foreseeable future.

And so, they optimize for staying alive. Their inertia and focus are to remain that way, and they try very hard to avoid making mistakes that might put that course of survival at risk.[58] Most people work at companies that are "default alive," and so most of the business strategy that we learn is optimized for companies that are "default alive." MBA programs are almost all tailored for companies that are "default alive."

Early stage companies, by contrast, are usually "default dead." Their expenses are greater than their revenue, and they are losing money. If things continue along the current trajectory, at some point in the reasonably near future, the company will run out of money, and the entrepreneur will be looking for a new job. Companies that are "default dead" have a different set of problems to solve, and their leaders face a different set of pressures.

57　Graham, Paul. "Default Alive or Default Dead?" Paul Graham. October 2015. http://www.paulgraham.com/aord.html.

58　This corporate instinct, combined with the instincts of the humans who work there to avoid risk to keep their job, is part of what makes corporate innovation so difficult.

Once I realized that most of my business education focused on "default alive" companies and wouldn't apply to the "default dead" world of startups, I started looking for advice that would be more useful. I wanted to understand how to prepare both my business and myself to exist and succeed in the world of "default dead." I wanted to figure out how to be more resilient.

I discovered that the most useful wisdom for companies that are "default dead" comes from studying people who find themselves personally in "default dead" scenarios. You see, most human beings live most of their lives as "default alive." If we continue along our current personal trajectory for the foreseeable future, we will continue to live. Yes, over some hazy time horizon, mortality looms for us all, but for the reasonably predictable future, we will continue to exist as humans. We are "default alive."

There are plenty of situations, however, where humans are suddenly thrust into situations where they become "default dead." Think of survivors on a lifeboat after their ship sinks, malnourished prisoners of war, or mountaineers at altitudes where oxygen doesn't support life. In these sorts of conditions, people fight for their daily survival, much like a startup.

Scientists have reached surprising conclusions about what differentiates those who live from those who die, conclusions that are tremendously helpful as we think about performing in an environment where the company is "default dead." In survival situations, the body immediately goes through all the stress reactions we talked about in previous chapters. Cortisol and adrenaline are dumped into the bloodstream, and the body's physiology responds accordingly with the adaptations we have discussed.

Most people quickly give in to these emotions and let them take over. They become panicked, frustrated, and react out of fear. They wallow in the discomfort and danger of their current situation, allowing the frustration to overwhelm them and adopting a victim posture about why they are stuck in this undesirable situation. They curse their environment and everything that has put them there, fixating on some time horizon where things will be better. "If we can just make it to that point on the horizon," they tell themselves, "the misery will be gone." Their fixation on the future overwhelms their ability to stay in the present.

Their minds and bodies react in predictable ways. They become less aware of their surroundings and less capable of processing information or thinking creatively. With their cerebral cortex overwhelmed by feelings of fear and anxiety, they can't clearly see what is around them. The Crocodile overwhelms the Philosopher. If they are in the situation with others, they usually begin thinking about "me versus them" and are accordingly less capable of teamwork or trust. They often make a bad situation worse as their bad decisions compound.

Lessons Of Survival

With some of those lessons and challenges in mind, I spent a lot of time studying survival. How do people survive, and what lessons can we apply to the world of the entrepreneur?

Surviving entrepreneurship is certainly different from surviving genocide—but there are lessons on cultivating resilience we can learn from extreme situations. Research into Holocaust survivors has identified patterns of behavior associated with survival and resilience.[59] The critical abilities were:

---

59   Greene, Roberta R., Hantman, Shira, Sharabi, Adi, Cohen, Harriet. "Holocaust Survivors: Three Waves of Resilience Research." National Library of Medicine. 2012. https://pubmed.ncbi.nlm.nih.gov/23092377/.

- Accepting a traumatic situation as being highly abnormal but temporary
- Maintaining positive social relationships and sense of belonging
- Cultivating optimism and unwavering belief that one will survive and return to a normal life
- Giving to others who are suffering when possible
- Expressing grief to accept, as much as possible, traumatic losses
- Identifying with something transcendent
- Accepting and reacting to change and the unpredictable

These individuals endured unimaginable adversity and years of fear and unrelenting uncertainty. We recognize now that embracing community, increasing our flexibility, leaning into our faith, experiencing our pain, and acknowledging that "this too, shall pass" can be protective.

Survivors stay focused on the present rather than allowing their mind to focus on the future. They keep their attention on the "here and now," finding ways to get comfortable in their current situation and even find beauty or joy in it, precarious though it may be. It seems almost strange, but they find opportunities for joy and happiness even as they face mortal danger.

In his book *Deep Survival,* Laurence Gonzales describes the importance of dark humor during dangerous times using the analogy of our mind being a horse that our consciousness is trying to jockey:

> That horse can either work for us or against us. It can win the race or explode in the gate. It is learning when to soothe

and gentle it and when to let it run that marks the winning jockey, the true survivor. And that is what the dark humor of various subcultures is all about: gentling the beast, keeping it cool; and when it's time to run, it's about letting it flow, having emotion and reason in perfect balance. That's what characterizes elite.

Developing a Training Plan

In the next few chapters, I'll lay out a series of suggestions to develop the resilience to survive in the journey. Much like reading a book about mountaineering or marathon running, this book can help you understand the concepts, but it will be your daily practice, not just the reading, that will build mental resilience. Reading the book helps you understand the concepts more quickly and potentially avoid common mistakes that may come from trial and error, but practicing those concepts builds the muscles to accomplish the task. You can't train for a marathon by reading books on marathon running; you can only train by doing.

Whether you think of yourself as a serial entrepreneur or someone focused on one particular idea, you are an *entrepreneur* the same way an NFL player is an *athlete*. To succeed, athletes must constantly hone and refine their bodies and focus on injury prevention. The sports world is full of incredibly talented athletes whose career ended tragically early because of injury. And while some injury is the result of luck and therefore unavoidable, there's no question that the right training can improve your odds of *being* lucky by making your body more resilient.

As an entrepreneur, your mind is the organ that's critical to your success. To succeed, you must hone and refine your mind to make better decisions under stress. Put another way, the most important determinant of the success of a company is the entrepreneur, and the most important quality of an entrepreneur is the optimal performance of their mind. Your mind is inevitably going to encounter several stressors as part of the process, so building your mental resilience to those stressors is critical to your success in the profession of entrepreneurship.

Just like an athlete's muscle mass and flexibility aren't built overnight, mental resiliency is a practice that develops over time as a result of training. There will be setbacks and challenges. Building mental resilience is like going to the gym. It's hard and uncomfortable at first, but over time it becomes habit, and you begin to miss the practice when you aren't doing it.

What I hope to impress upon you is that cultivating your mental resilience practice is the most important way to train to be an entrepreneur. It's no different than stretching or lifting weights to play football. Committing to a practice that develops mental resiliency is critical to entrepreneurial success.

Whether we are in the Delusions of Grandeur phase or The Death Zone of Imposter Syndrome, our job remains the same. Stay alive, don't quit, continue moving forward. Doing this sounds so easy, but doing it well ends up being surprisingly difficult.

As I read books and studies of humans beating the odds and surviving harrowing situations, I noticed the same themes kept popping up repeatedly. Whether in the context of military effectiveness, surviving the Holocaust, or making it off Everest alive in a storm, the same concepts kept reasserting themselves. Interestingly enough, these ideas didn't seem to be fads: they were consistent, from biblical stories to modern day research.

Defining The Resilience Cycle

There is a cycle of resilience for survivors, with three key steps.

- They prepare for the likelihood that things will go wrong and that the situation will get worse.
- They prioritize the important things and don't allow themselves to get sidetracked by distractions.
- They adapt to changes quickly by letting go of prior beliefs to deal with the current situation.[60]

Successful entrepreneurs are no different. The most successful entrepreneurs are constantly preparing for what comes next, ruthlessly prioritizing their time and resources to accomplish their goals, and adapting to rapidly changing and dynamic environments.

Sounds simple enough, right? If you want to be good at being an entrepreneur, make sure to prepare, prioritize, and adapt. Do those things well, and you'll be much better than the average entrepreneur. Except that most of us constantly get in our own way. Because we are human, we make very predictable mistakes that make it harder to go through the resilience cycle. The four most common and predictable mistakes are that we:

- Process new information poorly
- Fixate on past mistakes
- Perform activity for its own sake
- Focus our energy on the past or future

It's hard to prepare for the future when our minds are stuck in a shame loop relitigating past decisions. It's difficult to effectively prioritize while our Crocodile minds are playing tricks on us

---

60 Some readers will notice these concepts are similar to the OODA loop in military parlance (observe, orient, decide, act) or the unofficial slogan of the United States Marines: "Improvise, adapt, and overcome."

about what's important. It's impossible to adapt to the present state of affairs while we are living in a future fantasyland of happiness post-exit.

In the next few chapters, we are going to talk about the fundamental skills that differentiate excellent entrepreneurs and the abilities that enable those skills. The skills are practical things that you can execute, built around preparation, prioritization, and adaptability.

Underpinning those skills are four key abilities:

- Discernment: The ability to see what's actually there (avoiding cognitive biases and mental traps)
- Forgiveness: The ability to forgive yourself (avoiding blame and the fixation on past mistakes)
- Stillness: The ability to be quiet and thoughtful (avoiding becoming addicted to action for its own sake)
- Presence: The ability to stay in the current moment (avoiding the temptation to get caught up in the past or future)

Understanding and practicing these foundational abilities allows us to effectively prepare, prioritize, and adapt, which in turn makes us more resilient to the ups and downs and far better entrepreneurs. I say this with confidence because there's a tremendous amount of research that reinforces this notion, but even more because I have lived and observed it.

Resilience in Action

Prior to working at SpringCM, I never had a role model of what it meant to be a resilient entrepreneur. I had never known successful entrepreneurs who showed up each day able to keep things in perspective and manage their emotions. I modeled myself after these silly, media-created personas of what a "real entrepreneur" should be but hadn't read the research on what would truly make me effective as an entrepreneur and a leader. And so, I modeled myself after counterproductive caricatures because they were all I had ever known.

I finally got to observe real leadership when I took a job at SpringCM working with two of the most amazing leaders I have ever met. They weren't the "hustle harder" type, measuring their manhood by the number of hours spent at the desk. Instead, they showed up to work steady and inspiring, even in tough times. They are experts in adapting to changing circumstances and keeping their teams motivated and focused, even as everything around them shifts.

Let me tell you a little bit more about my experience. I was deep in a funk after SimpleRelevance failed and I was laid off from my next job. It was a dark time and place for me emotionally and psychologically. The parts of my psyche that always worried I wasn't good enough began to chirp loudly in my ear. Clearly, I wasn't good enough! I had failed at being an entrepreneur and then failed at being an employee.

And then I got a call from Dan Dal Degan. Dan had been a mentor and friend over the years and was preparing to take over as CEO of a Chicago technology company, SpringCM. He would be partnering with the current Founder and CEO, Greg "Buck" Buchholz, who was demoting himself to COO to bring Dan in.

I told them both I was skeptical that this could possibly work. Buck was used to being CEO, I still thought of myself as a CEO, and Dan would be the actual CEO. How could a mid-sized tech company possibly accommodate all those egos? Would we be at each other's throats? Seemed like a recipe for failure. If Dan and Buck had tried to fight a battle over who was the alpha male, we would have had a civil war in the C-Suite. It would have been miserable for the employees and led to a terrible outcome for the business.

Thankfully, Buck and Dan have the innate traits of survivors, not the silly need for ego-gratification that we so often confuse with leadership. I ended up learning lessons in leadership, and in particular, the survival mentality from them. Buck had founded the company fifteen years prior to my joining and had been through more than his share of ups, downs, and brushes with insolvency. What I noticed my first week at the office, and continued to be impressed by, was how loose Buck and Dan kept the place. Even as disasters popped up around us, they walked around the office making jokes, chatting with employees, and asking about their families. They found beauty and joy in the day-to-day of running the company, a joy that was infectious across our culture. It was the only company I've ever worked at where no one would think twice if the CEO was sitting in the lounge practicing guitar in the middle of the afternoon.

I don't mean to suggest we had the vibe of some new-age startup where we were all walking around barefoot and no one was expected to work. Nor am I saying they were naïve to the challenges or immune from the stresses. Quite the contrary; Buck and Dan understood our corporate survival hung in the balance almost every day. We had high expectations and held ourselves accountable.

But it was loose. It was relaxed. There was an expectation to perform, but it was clear that no one was going to perform better if we were all nervous or more stressed. And so, even as they were surprisingly transparent to the team about the challenges we all faced, they kept those challenges from overwhelming us by setting an example of coolness under pressure. The result of this was the most amazing work culture I have ever seen or been a part of. A collection of wonderfully talented people more excited to go to work than I ever thought possible.

This culture was the result of the survivor personalities of Dan and Buck. It's not being naïve to the struggles or ignoring the risks. Quite the opposite; the survivor has an exceptionally clear-eyed view of the risks and challenges. The survivor doesn't run from the challenges of the day by living in a future fantasy land when things might be better. Instead, the survivor exists in the present, looks the challenges directly in the eye, and laughs in the face of risk. In doing so, it sends a message to the entire team that there's nothing to fear. We are going to face and enjoy single every day on its own terms. We are going to be comfortable, happy, and joyful in the here and now. We aren't going to wait until after some exit or round of fundraising to savor the day.

Buck and Dan loved to tease me about my constant reading and how I would bring up a given book for pretty much any leadership topic. They were more "gut-feel" leaders, blessed with an innate and almost surreal amount of self-awareness and genuine self-confidence. Their survivor personalities came naturally to them in a way that it doesn't for most entrepreneurs.

It certainly didn't come naturally to me. I had to read more to understand how to manage my mind and needed role models to emulate. I had more insecurities to deal with and felt the Imposter Syndrome more viscerally when I was in The Death Zone. I naturally had more ego to get in the way of my leadership and found that I wasn't seeing things as clearly, nor was I laughing at or finding joy in the daily grind. I had more of a tendency to beat myself up over mistakes of the past and either dread or fantasize about the future.

And so, for those of us who weren't born with these talents like Buck or Dan, I developed a series of tools and training suggestions to develop the survivor mentality and the mental resiliency to succeed as an entrepreneur.

Prepare

As we have already discussed, entrepreneurial success tends to not go in a nice line up and to the right. It's going to be rocky, uneven, and full of wild swings up and down. And yet, we so often treat entrepreneurial challenges as though they are case studies in optimizing efficiency for an MBA paper rather than the tooth and nail fight for survival that they actually are.

A great example of this is how we think about raising money. I have sat on many panels with well-meaning, successful folks where the question of "should I raise money" and "how much money should I raise" came up. The answer to these questions is usually some combination of explaining the math with the pre- and post-money valuations. There is usually a story of some poor schmuck who sells his company for $250 million and only owns 5 percent of it, leaving him with a measly $12.5 million—which is contrasted with a smarter entrepreneur who owned 50 percent of a $100 million dollar exit and walked away with $50 million. The meaning of this discussion is clear, and all the smart students walk away thinking to themselves that they need to be very conservative and thoughtful in how they raise money, lest they end up like that moron who only had 5 percent by the time he exited.

I know the audience walks away thinking that, because I listened to those talks and heard those stories more times than I could count. I internalized that advice. And because of that, I made one of the worst mistakes an entrepreneur can make. I didn't raise money when it was readily available to me.

The math example above discussing "would you rather own 5 percent or 50 percent" is correct, but the choice in this case is idiotic, because the frame of reference is all skewed. In that example, there's an implicit assumption that the entrepreneur will succeed and exit, with the question being how to optimize returns at the time of exit.

Entrepreneurship isn't a math problem, my friends. Optimizing on the math at exit is the exact wrong way to think about the problem. A much better frame of reference is to consider this to be a fight for survival, and how do you best prepare your company (and yourself) to survive?

I advise entrepreneurs to prepare for their journey by thinking of capital the way that I thought about oxygen on a mountaineering expedition. You want to store as much of it as possible but use as little as you can. Make sure that you have access to more if you start to get low. Recognize that more oxygen allows you to move faster and to think more clearly. It takes the pressure off, gives you more optionality, and allows you to stay at altitude much longer.

And, yes, there are certain mountaineers that climb some of the world's highest peaks without oxygen. Occasionally, an amateur mountaineer will even do the same thing. It can be done, it has been done, and there is a whole different level of glory associated with it. But climbing without oxygen also has a much higher fatality rate and leaves the climber with much less margin for error.

In the same way, some entrepreneurs will build great businesses without a capital cushion. It's possible and may lead to a larger financial exit, but it also dramatically increases the odds of failure if things don't go exactly according to plan.

But preparation isn't just about raising money. Preparing for the journey means building a network of advisors to help you when things go wrong. It means discussing the journey ahead with your partner to make sure they're aligned with the mission. Preparation is the opposite of Mount Stupid; it's the realization that you have imperfect knowledge about the challenges to come and putting yourself in a position to be resilient to those challenges. Remember that the most basic way to succeed as an entrepreneur is to stay alive, not quit, and keep moving in the right direction. Preparation is the act of anticipating anything that might get in the way.

Prepare for and expect things to go wrong. Expect hires to not work out. Expect people to get sick. Expect customers to cancel for reasons you don't understand. Expect competitors to enter your market and the competitive dynamics to shift overnight. Expect people to make mistakes. Expect investors to renege on commitments. Expect things to go wrong throughout the journey, and you're unlikely to be disappointed. If you expect and prepare for these contingencies with a plan to see you through the hard times, you are never going to regret it.

Prioritize

Perhaps the defining activity of entrepreneurship is the constant striving to accomplish great things with limited resources. Because of this, prioritization is the constant struggle. I think that's the reason phrases like "hustle harder" or "do more, faster" are so common in entrepreneurial lingo. It's a lazy way to advise someone who has more work to do than time to do that work. As we have talked about, that advice breaks under examination and often leaves you worse off for having listened to it.

In fact, perhaps the greatest temptation of the entrepreneur is to take all the various tasks of the company upon her shoulders. Entrepreneurs know the buck stops with us, and so we too often try to take on every task! I also think, if we're being totally honest, we at times bury ourselves in work to avoid the tasks that we want to avoid. I would find myself arguing technical points with my CTO for hours instead of raising money, which would have been a better use of my time. It's much easier to ignore critical issues if you fill every waking hour with other work that needs to be done. We subconsciously avoid the things that are most important by busying ourselves with nonstop activity.

As with most of the lessons in this book, I learned this one the hard way. Venture Capitalist Fred Wilson has written some of the best advice on this topic. He writes,[61] "A CEO does only three things. Sets the overall vision and strategy of the company and communicates it to all stakeholders. Recruits, hires, and retains the very best talent for the company. Makes sure there is always enough cash in the bank."

If you're like I was, you will read that quote, nod appreciatively, and say what a smart guy Wilson is. And then, you'll immediately go back to a calendar full of other things besides the priorities Wilson calls out. You'll do a product review, take a customer call, talk with a couple prospects, review a partnership agreement, and develop plans for an upcoming conference. We *say* we will prioritize strategy, recruiting, and fundraising, but then we don't let ourselves off the hook by doing "only" those three jobs. We force so much more onto our plate.

---

61   Wilson, Fred. "What A CEO Does." AVC. August 30, 2010. https://avc.com/2010/
     08/what-a-ceo-does/.

The problem is that by busying ourselves with all kinds of other work, we create the opportunity for our minds to avoid those critical tasks. The key to prioritizing time is learning the ability to say "yes" to the most important tasks on our list and "no" to the rest. For most of us this is hard...we like saying yes! We like pleasing others, we like taking more upon our shoulders. *Yes* feels great. *No* is uncomfortable.

For the rest of your entrepreneurial career, you will have more work to do than you will have time to do it. The only way to solve for this is ruthless prioritization. Strategy, people, and cash. If you solve for those three things, the rest of the business will take care of itself. If you succumb to the temptation of distraction, you risk taking your focus from the things that matter most.

Adapt

There is no profession where the rules change faster than being an entrepreneur. We exist in dynamic environments that are in a state of constant flux. Some of us decide we will find a way to control everything, as though our sheer desire can bend the universe to our will. Others recognize there are a lot of things they can't change and focus on adapting quickly.

I'll confess that I was, unfortunately, in the first group as an entrepreneur. While I tried to keep a loose office and have my team celebrate wins, that celebration was always rooted in *intensity* and competition, not in joyful play. The idea of "play" would have seemed silly to me. Childlike, naïve, ridiculous. Not like the serious entrepreneur that I considered myself to be. I was much more deeply steeped in the idea of "hustle harder" than I was "enjoy the day for its own sake."

Accordingly, I fixated on a lot of future goals. I thought a lot about how happy I would be when the company raised more money or when I could hire people with more experience. I got excited about some point in the future when the pressure would be off. What I found was that my fixation on the future was kind of like those "free beer tomorrow" signs you see in bars. No matter what I accomplished, that mythical moment when the pressure would be off never arrived. But that intensity just seemed like what "real entrepreneurs" bring to the office every day.

The best survivors, and the best entrepreneurs, constantly adapt to their changing circumstances. They don't allow themselves to get caught up in the temptation of how they want the world to be, but instead they focus on it for what it is. They don't worry about the past, and they let the future take care of itself. Instead, they focus all their time and energy on the present, influencing what they can to improve their odds of success.

There is a subtlety here that is important to understand. At first blush, "stay present and don't fixate on the future" seems like it could be the opposite of the idea of "planning" or the idea of "visualizing what you want the future to be." The difference is intention. Taking time to contemplate and plan for the future is a very valuable thing to do! That's very different from "living in the future" with your mind, fantasizing to escape the present.

Preparing, prioritizing, and adapting all sound easy enough; none of these are particularly controversial ideas. Unfortunately, we often get in our own way when we try to do these things. We have a tough time seeing the world for what it is, avoiding the temptation to constantly relive our past mistakes, embracing stillness and introspection, or being present in the moment.

And so, as the pressures of the entrepreneurial journey mount, we unwittingly sabotage the skills we need to excel as survivors and entrepreneurs. In the next four chapters, I'll unpack each of these abilities in more detail and suggest exercises to develop them with the goal of allowing ourselves to more effectively prepare, prioritize, and adapt.

LESSON FROM MOUNT EVEREST

Part of my mental resilience training for Everest included visualizing my "climbing persona"—how did I want to be perceived by my teammates on the mountain? How did I want them to feel about me, how did I want to come across? What sort of effect would I want to be known for? How could I improve my odds and those of my team to succeed?

I decided I was going to focus on being the "grinning idiot." I was going to try to be happy, no matter the situation. I knew there would be challenges and frustrations, but I also knew that complaining can be contagious. The more I allowed dissatisfaction to seep into my thoughts and language, the more it would reinforce whatever negativity the rest of the group was harboring. I decided I would make a conscious effort to be the voice of positivity and try to be remembered for my optimism.

I have no idea how my teammates actually remember me, but I felt like I did a pretty good job of maintaining that positive point of view. Whether it was food, illness, injury, or anything else, I tried to look on the bright side and keep smiling, joking, laughing, and celebrating. I was trying to make a focused effort to adopt the persona of a survivor, even if I didn't always naturally feel it.

It worked for me. One of the best compliments I have ever received came from Suvash Dawadi, a doctor with the Everest ER[62] who became a friend thanks to the amount of time I spent in the medical tent. There are no HIPAA privacy laws in Nepal, and so Suvash decided to share his perspective on my climb with the world on Facebook:

> Erik Severinghaus climbed Everest with International Mountain Guides. He fought Traveler's Diarrhea right from the beginning of the season and kept having loose motions throughout the season despite the best of efforts by Everest ER docs. However, he made it to the top without a complaint and came back to us smiling.

When Suvash saw me as that picture was taken, I'll never forget him looking at me and saying, "You are the strongest bull I have ever seen!" This from a man who treats the best athletes in the world on the most amazing of adventures at EBC.

To be clear, I'm not the strongest climber, and I am objectively less strong and accomplished than many others who were on the mountain that year. I am absolutely convinced that the strength to climb was there *because of the smile*. Adopting the smiling, joyful attitude of the survivor allowed me to get every last bit of performance out of my body.

---

62   If you're interested in learning more about the amazing doctors on Everest, I recommend this article by Suvash. https://www.outdoorjournal.com/news-2/everest-er-medicine-at-top-of-the-world/. You can also learn more about the Himalayan Rescue Organization at https://himalayanrescue.org.np/.

TAKEAWAY FOR ENTREPRENEURSHIP

Developing a survivor's mentality is all about the mindset you bring to the challenge. How you mentally approach the hardest journeys of your life will have a material impact on whether or not you succeed.

JOURNAL PROMPT

What traits of a survivor do you identify with that come naturally to you? Which ones do you anticipate needing more time and energy to develop?

Discernment:
The Ability to Truly
See What Is There

I'll never forget how close my good friend came to a life threatening snakebite on the first day of an easy backpacking trip.

I was on the Appalachian Trail with my good friend Scott. We were miles away from the nearest road or town, chatting as we stopped for lunch, taking in the sunshine and beautiful scenery. We were relaxed, happy, and enjoying ourselves; our guard was down. Suddenly, in the same instant, I grabbed him, and he jumped back. The moment after we reacted, I heard a rattle, looked down, and saw a rattlesnake primed to strike. As we backed away, the snake slithered off, and that was that.

What I will never forget about the experience is that we each reacted before we had consciously seen or heard the snake. I wasn't aware of any mental processing that caused my arm to reach out, my heart rate to increase, or Scott to jump back. It had all happened without conscious thought. Given the potential consequences of a venomous snakebite, miles from the nearest road, the speed of that reaction might have saved Scott's life.

While that experience with the snake has only happened once, I have probably had thousands of experiences where I briefly see something like a stick out of the corner of my eye that I think might be a snake, felt my heartbeat kick up, and then realized it was no big deal. The fact that my brain overreacts a thousand times and mistakes a stick for a snake has no real cost to my body. Sure, it stresses me out for split second, my heart races, and it's annoying. But, if my mind wasn't always primed to overreact to an unexpected threat, Scott could have died.

My mind's willingness to overreact and assume that even something as harmless as a stick might be a mortal threat is no accident. Our minds are constantly observing our environment, and when there's ambiguity we prime ourselves for a worst-case scenario until proven otherwise. That tendency to overreact literally saves lives. Remember, from an evolutionary standpoint, our mind's primary job is to keep our body alive so we can pass down our DNA. With that being the goal, our minds haven't evolved to see what is actually in front of us. Our minds have evolved to anticipate the worst possible threat and to engage our response systems at the first sign of danger. The mind errs on the side of caution and only disarms the alert systems when certain the threat has abated.

In the snake example, my subconscious was constantly process-ing the visual inputs, noticed a pattern match for "looks like snake," and immediately acted. The Crocodile in my brain didn't wait to confirm with the Philosopher. Before either of us had processed the information or communicated, Scott and I were both ready to fight or flee.

That interplay between the Crocodile and Philosopher is con-stant in our minds. While we like to think that the Philosopher of our cerebral cortex drives most of our thinking and activity, the fierce Crocodile of the limbic system has his own tricks to get what he wants. We have already talked about the most obvious one, which is that in certain scenarios it assumes control over the activity, short-circuits the mind, and acts. Remember that the limbic system is wrapped around the brain stem, and that Crocodile brain can take action without permission from the more high-minded cortex.

In most cases, however, it's more subtle than that. The Crocodile of the limbic system acts as the operator in a game of telephone, passing information between your senses and your logical brain. And the Crocodile is not an honest broker. He quietly manipulates information to get what he wants.

I'll give you a personal example of this dynamic in action. Years ago, I was in a relationship with a perfectionist, and I would be asked to do basic housework like vacuuming or wiping off the coun-tertop. Inevitably that housework wasn't done up to her standards, and she would berate me, sometimes for minutes or even hours at a time. She would cry and lecture me on my shortcomings. Through tears, she would tell me that, clearly, I didn't care enough about her to do the task right. I felt like I let her down, and somehow an imperfectly cleaned counter left me feeling shame, frustration, guilt, and self-loathing. I can be a sensitive guy, and those episodes left scars that went deep.

Fast-forward a few years to my present-day marriage with a loving and supporting wife who appreciates my attempts at housework and is thankful for them. She has never once berated me for not acting up to her standards. My logical brain knows that there is no threat to me like there used to be.

And yet, to this day I have a physical reaction when she asks me to wipe down the countertop. I feel my heart rate skip up, and I feel myself growing irritable and defensive. Before my brain has even processed the words she says, my body is primed for fight or flight. I'm a 250-pound adult who has climbed Mount Everest, and my body still instinctively reacts to this gentle request like a scared child.

In that moment, I overreact because of something that's not actually there. What is in front of my eyes is a well-meaning, loving, and supportive wife who is asking me to help with a trivial chore. What I'm "seeing," what my body is reacting to, is years of toxic emotion buried deep in my psyche. Before the Philosopher of my cortex is able to rationally analyze the request, the Crocodile of my limbic system is already baring his teeth, ready to either attack or escape. This subtle manipulation of our sensory input and our physical reaction happens all the time. Once I learned to recognize and track my subconscious reactions, I found dozens every day.

Having the Crocodile between the senses and the Philosopher makes tremendous sense for the jungle-combat environments in which our brains evolved. Without that Crocodile running interference, Scott might have died of a snakebite. But, dammit if that Crocodile doesn't make it a lot harder to be a thoughtful, loving, and supportive partner to my wife!

In the same way that the Crocodile of the limbic system hijacks my thinking and makes it tougher to be a husband, he makes it so much harder to be an entrepreneur. He sees threats everywhere. And while the Philosopher would happily debate the truth or fiction of various observations, the Crocodile colors the information being passed along and simply hijacks thinking without ever making it explicit.

Unfortunately, this dynamic isn't limited to hiking trips or relationships. Thanks to the emotional reactions of my limbic system, as an entrepreneur I became unconsciously convinced of a great number of things that in hindsight were just not true. I'll give you a few examples:

- My limbic system would tune out well-meaning and thoughtful advice from seasoned advisers to protect me from some imagined hurt or rejection.

- My identity was dependent upon me being a Founder/ CEO—a successful one. So, while I might intellectually be aware that my profession as an entrepreneur is but one part of my whole self, my limbic system associated threats to the business with threats to my very person.

- I hired a bad CTO who isolated my technical team from the business and caused them to eventually quit en masse. I didn't want to face the reality that I had made a bad hire, so I didn't fix the situation until it was almost too late, and I nearly lost my entire team.

I could go on, but you get the point. In each of these scenarios, I wasn't seeing what was truly there. I couldn't bring myself to face the facts as they *actually* were, and so I subconsciously ignored data or looked the other way, which led to making bad decisions.

The key to overcoming this is learning to work with the Crocodile instead of against him. There are two time-honored techniques for this. These can be done by yourself in real time, in a journal, or in conversations with a mentor or a therapist.

The first key is to break the situation/emotion/interpretation feedback loop. Remember that information comes in through your brain stem and passes through your limbic system before it reaches your cortex. If you ignore the existence of the Crocodile, he will color all the information with his own interpretation, which will generally be angry, fearful, aggressive, or contain a host of strong and repressed emotions. When you feel yourself starting to engage emotionally, stop and take a deep breath. Now, ask yourself, what's the story you are telling yourself that's causing the emotions? In effect, interrogate the Crocodile. In my example about wiping the countertop, I had to ask the Crocodile several times to finally figure out why I was reacting the way I did.

The second key is to reduce the conflict between the Crocodile and Philosopher. Pet the Crocodile, thank him, and soothe him. Like everyone else, I often felt emotions I'd recognize as irrational, and my go-to move was always to ignore them. I knew it was dumb to get upset about being asked to wipe the countertop; I didn't know why I felt that way, and so I would try to ignore or suppress the emotional reaction. Unfortunately, the Crocodile is crafty and always finds a way to avoid being ignored. I might be able to respond nicely to the request to wipe down the countertop, but I would usually feel threatened and find some way to act out later in the evening. And so, rather than ignoring that limbic warning, I acknowledge it and thank it. Literally. "Thank you, Mr. Crocodile. Your defense mechanisms kept me safe when I was in a bad situation, and I appreciate that. This situation is okay though; I'm safe, so it's fine."

Now that we have discussed these techniques in theory, let's apply them to four common entrepreneurial experiences.

Taking Feedback Without Becoming Defensive

While you're in the Delusions of Grandeur part of the journey, your Crocodile is constantly primed to fend off negative feedback to protect the ego. Unfortunately, the people who are probably the best equipped to help you are people that will offer you candid feedback, which usually isn't all positive. The best mentors are the ones who respect you enough to tell it to you straight, but that's only valuable if you can control the Crocodile long enough to let the Philosopher listen intellectually.

As usual, I have a personal story on this topic. As I met with investors trying to raise money, I pitched a very well-regarded local angel investor. I desperately wanted him to invest, not only because of his capital, but also because his investment would be a signal of strength to other local investors and VCs. He gave me some great critical feedback that I listened to, but I stopped following up with him after a couple meetings. I'm not sure exactly why, but I think I was intimidated by him and afraid to continue the discussion. Since I couldn't stomach asking him for advice, I was certainly too scared to ask him to invest and risk his rejection. I just went dark on him.

A year later, after I had closed my investment round, we ran into each other. He congratulated me on the round and asked me if he had accidentally offended me. I told him no, that I really respected him and asked why he might have thought as much. He responded that he couldn't understand why I had stopped following up and never even asked him to invest! He felt left out since I had closed a funding round without him. My dream investor was eager to be involved! But I couldn't see that in the moment with my Crocodile trying to protect my psyche from the fear of rejection. I didn't see what was in front of my face, overreacted to a threat that didn't even exist, and missed an incredible opportunity!

Homework

Ask someone you trust for critical feedback about your company, your leadership, or another topic you feel sensitive about. Interrogate your emotions with that person, to yourself, or in a journal after. Did you feel upset? Defensive? Did you want to tune out? Did your heart rate jump? Did your stomach churn? Why is that? What is your Crocodile trying to protect you from? What would that feedback say about you? Now, thank your Crocodile for protecting you, but remind him that you really need to hear that information if you're going to succeed.

Contemplating Failing Without Being a Failure

The thing that makes The Death Zone of Imposter Syndrome so toxic is the combination of the stress we feel and our tendency to associate our entire sense of self with our company. If you are like most entrepreneurs, the concept of your company failing is a fear that can't even be contemplated. It's the terror that dare not speak its name. Somewhere, your Philosopher is aware that the most likely statistical outcome for your business is failure, but your Crocodile absolutely refuses to acknowledge that as even a remote possibility. When the Philosopher and the Crocodile are in disagreement, we feel tremendous stress and anxiety that we may have a tough time recognizing or acknowledging.

We must reconcile the two parts of our brain and the competing notions. We do that by using our Philosopher to interrogate the Crocodile; in effect, we look fear in the eye. Fear that sits in the limbic system unsurfaced and unspoken has an ability to control us. As soon as we recognize that fear, acknowledge, and interrogate it, the power goes away.

Let's acknowledge the fear and say the thing that is unsaid. Statistically speaking, the most likely outcome of starting a new company is failure. Period. Full stop. I know it's disheartening, but it's just math, and it doesn't mean that you won't succeed.

Similarly, when I went to Everest, I was aware that the most likely outcome of the journey was that I would *not* summit. Most people who try to climb Everest don't succeed, especially on their first try. That failure may happen because of weather, injury, sickness, or simply bad luck. No matter how hard I trained, my most likely outcome was failure.

Note that this is the opposite of what so many people would advise. "Tough guys" will counsel you to ignore the fear with useless mantras like "failure is not an option." Your Crocodile is too smart for that sort of reductionist stupidity. Failure is an option! It is statistically the most likely option. Part of your mind already knows it to be true, so let's just acknowledge the elephant in the room.

In the back of my mind, I always knew failure was an option, but it was an option that terrified me. And so, for a long time as an entrepreneur, I avoided learning from other entrepreneurs who had failed. If you asked me, I probably wouldn't have said I "judged" them, but I definitely had an aversion to talking with the "Failures." Looking back, I suppose I assigned some sort of moral failing to anyone who didn't succeed, and I reacted to what I feared in myself. I never had much of a conversation about entrepreneurial failure with anyone who had been through it.

I finally got a glimpse behind that curtain when I caught up with a friend of mine named Justin Massa.[63] From the moment I met Justin and through the years that I have known him, he's always been one of the "good guys." Brilliant, charismatic, amazing sense of humor. The kind of person you want to be around. As it happens, Justin is also a failed entrepreneur.

Justin had founded a company called FoodGenius and raised millions of dollars of investment. For a time, his was one of the hottest companies in Chicago. Alas, after years spent building the company, he had a rocky exit. The company "sold," but it wasn't a terribly lucrative sale. Plus, he had also already left his role as CEO, partially at the suggestion of his Board. It wouldn't be completely accurate to say he got fired and the company was put through a fire-sale, but that description is pretty close to the truth. So, while there are always some shades of gray, Justin's tenure could be judged a failure.

I didn't really know how to reconcile my admiration for him with his failure. How could someone I looked up to—one of the "good guys" I aspired to emulate—not succeed? While I knew the statistics, I didn't think they applied to me or people that I revered. I always assumed that *we* would succeed, some other folks would be those statistical failures. Justin was supposed to be one of the winners—the same way I was!

But he wasn't one of the winners. To make matters worse, I was no longer sure SimpleRelevance was going to be one of the winners

---

63   It only further speaks to Justin's character and sense of self that he asked that I not anonymize this anecdote as I originally intended.

either. When Justin and I sat down at a local dive bar, I had a few things on my mind. Certainly, I wanted to see how my friend was doing and offer help if I could. Selfishly, I wanted to know what I was in for as I contemplated my own failure. I assumed it must be some horrible and barren wasteland, some lesser circle of hell that forever torments the soul. I was ready to hear the details from him.

I had so many questions. Had his friends abandoned him? Did his wife look at him with disappointment in her eyes? Was he now an unemployable pariah? Did the people in his life still love and care about him? Was he about to be broke? Did he feel like he needed to leave Chicago and start over?

As we sat at the bar and he told me his story, a surprising scene unfolded. He told me how he had been able to re-connect with his wife and actually spend time with his family. They had recently gone on a vacation, and he didn't even check his email. He told me about getting six-figure job offers that seemed interesting and fulfilling and how confident he was that he'd soon be getting paid to work. Rather than soul-crushing torment, Justin had never been happier!

Not everyone's journey ends exactly the way Justin's did, and the post-exit process can be difficult. I was laid off less than a year after my exit, proving that even when you think you have hit rock bottom, you may yet have further to fall. But I, too, went on to experience some of the happiest days of my life after the failure of SimpleRelevance.

The moral of the story is that the failure of your company probably isn't the catastrophe you might imagine. Most entrepreneurs who return to the world of employment find themselves sought after for their demonstrated courage, not ostracized for their self-perceived failure. If you look squarely at the risk of failure, you are almost certain to find that it's not nearly as bad as the unspoken fear lurking somewhere in your mind.

It's important to talk to others in your life to address the risk of failure head-on. Before I ever took money from friends or family, I made sure to ask them, "How will you feel about me if we fail as a company and I don't return any of your capital?" If they'd be angry about me losing their money despite hard work and executing with integrity, I didn't want their cash. Similarly, ask your partner how they'll feel about you if you fail. You'll almost certainly learn that they'll love you regardless of the financial outcome, but hearing them say it explicitly can be tremendously validating to your psyche.

You'll recall that The Death Zone struggle comes from the stress of believing that we can't live up to the expectations of others. We naturally try to solve that problem by being better entrepreneurs, always trying to figure out a way to live up to those expectations. There's an even more important way to reduce that stress, realizing the fallacy of trying to be who we think everyone else wants us to be. We need to recognize that others may have far different expectations than we think and that their expectations of us usually have to do more with their own issues than with us.

When I told my investors that I wouldn't be returning capital to them as part of the SimpleRelevance acquisition, all but one of them were supportive and positive. They almost all told me how much they appreciated my effort, hard work and energy. They could not have been kinder, and they'll probably never know how much that kindness meant to me. I'll never forget the VC who responded to me that his only request was to be able to invest in the next company and the one after that, telling me he wanted to buy the Erik Severinghaus index fund.

There was one exception to the rule of kindness and human generosity I saw during that dark time. One investor pushed for a hard shutdown of the company through bankruptcy rather than the soft landing we negotiated that was better for our employees, customers, the bank, and virtually every other stakeholder. One investor who sent me a letter making his contempt clear, telling me in no uncertain terms that I was an embarrassment to him and the worst investment he had ever made.

As you can imagine, that letter wounded me deeply and infuriated me. I felt like he wasn't just kicking me while I was down but was stomping on what tiny ember of dignity remained in my soul. It took a long time for me to process those feelings and realize that his behavior was a result of *his* problems, not mine. He was rich beyond most people's wildest dreams but had to make himself feel better by stomping on an entrepreneur during his hardest time.

As an entrepreneur, you're going to see that people project themselves onto you. Most of them will be kind and generous, thoughtful, and helpful. Some will flatter and suck up to you. Some will steal from you. A few will be mean-spirited and try to tear you down or kick you in your time of need. The important thing is to recognize that they are simply being who *they* are, and that it has little or nothing to do with who you are.

Homework

Talk to a couple people you know and respect who have had a company fail. Ask them how they feel about themselves now versus before the failure. Ask them what their finances are like, how much time they get to spend time with their family, and how they'd rate their stress level. Ask what the silver linings were and whether they now regret what transpired at that time.

Confront Your Financial Realities

One of the most frustrating perversities of entrepreneurship, especially in early stages of the journey, is that you probably will work harder than you have ever worked and yet feel poorer by the day. While I was building SimpleRelevance, I also co-founded a franchise company that built seven Papa John's Pizza locations in Chicago. As a starving entrepreneur, or at least one who felt broke given my wild swings in paper wealth, it turned out to be quite strategic to be an owner of my local pizza restaurant. Free pizza is an amazing perk no matter who you are, but especially if you're having a shit day and feeling broke. I took full advantage, getting absurd quantities of chain pizza delivered to the apartment and devouring it for breakfast, lunch, and dinner.[64]

During this period of dual ownership, I felt like I was constantly losing cash. In theory, my companies were building asset value, but it doesn't feel that way when your bank account is dwindling daily. I vividly remember getting pizza delivered one evening and giving the delivery guy a good tip. His eyes lit up, and he thanked me profusely.[65] What occurred to me in that moment was the fact that this driver was putting in an honest day's work and would be taking home an honest day's pay. He was happy, and his net worth had

---

64 When "Papa John" Schnatter and the brand came into conflict, he claimed to have eaten fifty pizzas in thirty days as an exercise in quality control. The world was aghast at his gluttony, but I think I might have already broken his record with my own exercise in expense management!

65 Even if you feel poor, there's really no excuse to be a bad tipper when you're the owner and the pizza is free.

gone up as a result going to work that day. He had some amount of cash flow for his efforts.

Contrast that with my last few months of not getting paid, and in fact pouring my personal savings into the business just to make payroll. I had no idea if I'd ever get a paycheck from the work I was doing, and each day my bank account got smaller. I was working hellacious hours and went home exhausted and poorer for the work I had done. I really envied the delivery guy in that moment and everyone who was actually getting paid for the work they did, ending each month with more rather than less money.

If your eyes are rolling as you read this, I get it. My Philosopher brain agrees with you. I had never walked a mile in that delivery driver's shoes and have no idea what stresses and pressures he was under. It felt silly to me at the time to acknowledge those emotions, and it still feels silly writing about them many years later. But the Crocodile brain of my limbic system felt that way in the moment. From my disjointed perspective, it felt like the delivery driver's income was somewhat predictable while mine was gyrating like the EKG of someone undergoing defibrillation. My emotional self craved stability and predictability.

One of my biggest mistakes was, in identifying myself with my company, I implicitly decided I would backstop the company with every dollar I had in the bank. To me, that was just what an "all in" entrepreneur was supposed to do, a notion I'm sure I learned from the Entrepreneurial Advice Industry. Like so many relationships in life, when I didn't articulate boundaries, I left myself vulnerable and feeling taken advantage of.

To make matters worse, I would avoid bad news by avoiding looking at my finances. I had a vague notion that I had enough money in the bank to get through the next month or two, so I reasoned that my best move was to avoid the stress of confronting the problem head on.

Of course, avoiding the problem never actually relieves the stress associated with it. It's still there, lurking, and becomes even more powerful when it's unacknowledged.

Homework

The pressure of the financial sacrifices we make in the journey become less potent when we confront them. Walk through your worst-case financial scenario in a journal or with a loved one. Remove the ambiguity around how long you can responsibly continue the entrepreneurial journey. Talk about additional sources of income or savings, and set explicit goals for both your corporate and personal liquidity. If you're willing to backstop the company with additional personal money, put that into a separate bank account and consider it already out the door.

Then, contemplate a world in which the company has undergone the worst failure imaginable. How long can you live on your personal savings? When would you need to look at other employment options? What would you do? Would you travel? Spend time with your family? What does that period of time look like? Visualizing and confronting the potential removes the ambiguity and much of the stress of the situation.

See Through the Eyes of Others

I have found the surest way to gain insight about my own situation is to counsel others on their problems. Without fail, as I ramble on trying to find something smart to say, I'll end up processing what should have been obvious insights about some problem that I'm going through. I usually just need to get out of my own head long enough to see things clearly and get some perspective.

While I was CEO of SimpleRelevance, I was fortunate enough to join a peer group of CEOs through a program modeled after the Young President's Organization's (YPO) forum exercise. About a dozen of us met every six weeks for four hours, which at the time I made the commitment, sounded like an insane amount of time to devote to this "soft stuff." I was so naïve and arrogant that I had to be cajoled into joining. I may not have thought that I knew *everything*, but I didn't think I had much to learn from a bunch of other entrepreneurs who I didn't consider successes yet.

When I joined that peer group, I quickly reassessed my opinion and developed a tremendous amount of respect for the other CEOs. They were all smart, ambitious, and generally really impressive men.[66] I went from thinking I was superior to feeling honored to be included amongst their ranks and excited to learn from them.

Time and again, I came to our meetings fixated on my own problems and convinced that, while I was clearly unworthy of running my company, these other entrepreneurs probably had it all figured out. I was about to lose my biggest customer. My funding might run out in four months. An employee I wanted just turned me down. I was having problems in my relationship.

And then everyone else would share. They had deaths in the family. Their marriages were on the rocks. Their kids were in really bad places psychologically. Their most important investor had just reneged on a term sheet. Their company was facing massive layoffs

---

66   Yes…men…. Unfortunately there wasn't a lot of diversity.

or the threat of going out of business completely. The list of challenges went on and on.

While I may not have loved or respected myself enough to give myself the benefit of the doubt, it was easy to see *their* problems didn't exist because *they* were bad entrepreneurs. These people I respected so much weren't struggling because they were dumb or lazy. Of course, they had their flaws, but these were all very impressive entrepreneurs! I began to understand that their challenges were part of the journey and not manifestations of their inadequacies. I finally put together that if that was true for them, it was probably also true for me. The only way I could forgive *myself*—even just a tiny bit—was through the context of *their* challenges.

There are lots of different entrepreneurial groups to join; some are formal and expensive, others informal and free. Some are large (ten to twelve people) while other groups are no more than two people who regularly meet at a bar. Two new fantastic online resources have recently emerged, Founders First[67] and Econa,[68] to build communities and help entrepreneurs confront their challenges.

Whether you choose a large, formal, and expensive group or simply have a standing reservation for a couple stools at the bar with a fellow entrepreneur, there are three qualities that distinguish the successful groups and make them valuable:

- Context—the group is made up of people who are living similar experiences and journeys so that their experiences add perspective to yours.
- Consistency—the group makes time to meet consistently even though everyone is busy.

---

67   https://www.foundersfirstsystem.com/.
68   https://econa.net/.

- Confidentiality—what is said is held in complete confidentiality and everyone can trust that.

Homework

How will you develop your peer support group? Would you consider joining an already established network like YPO,[69] Entrepreneur's Organization[70] (EO), or Vistage?[71] Or would you prefer a less formal group? How will you ensure you have people you can meet with consistently to add context to your situation and do so confidentially? How will you prioritize this commitment?

LESSON FROM MOUNT EVEREST

Most epic Mount Everest stories are about summit day and the heroic triumph of man over nature to reach the highest point in the world. I won't pass up the opportunity to share my summit story, but the hardest part of the climb for me was actually weeks before summit day on my first climb to Camp 3.

The Death Zone metaphor in this book comes from the mountaineering term for what happens to the body above 26,000 feet. At that altitude, your body is starved of oxygen, and your tissues begin to physically break down. While I experienced all of the physical symptoms, it wasn't my herniated disc, weeks of gastrointestinal distress, or almost collapsing from heat stroke that nearly ended the climb. I came close to quitting and ending my quest prematurely because I couldn't clearly see my own demons and face my lack of

---

69   https://www.ypo.org/.
70   https://www.eonetwork.org/.
71   https://www.vistage.com/.

self-confidence. My feeling of Imposter Syndrome came *this close* to overwhelming me. Of course, I didn't see it that way at the time.

I'll never forget that day. My group began our first climb from Camp 2 (21,000 feet) to Camp 3 (23,600 feet).[72] We started the climb at about 5 a.m.; it was dark and freezing cold. I sat at the breakfast table, trying to choke down some peanut butter toast, but it was hard to eat. Even though my body was working so much harder at altitude, my digestive system was a wreck, and it was tough for me to force food into my mouth and down my throat.

Our guides delivered the briefing the day before and told us to expect six hours of climbing. It was going to be a tough day, but I had no reason to believe it would be much tougher than any other. In preparing for my climb up Mount Everest, I read dozens of Everest accounts about the dangers of the Khumbu icefall and of summit day. I can't remember a single story that calls out the climb from Camp 2 to Camp 3 as anything but "just another day" on the mountain. Plus, I was usually climbing an hour or two ahead of schedule. I figured if we left by 6 a.m. that I'd be in camp by noon.

I went through my checklist, and we set out. By this point, the pre-climb checklist had become routine, so while I was rushing a bit to make sure I left camp with everyone else, it was a pretty typical pre-climb morning.

Typical, that is, until we got about thirty minutes out of camp. As we made a quick stop to put on crampons, I realized I only had one water bottle. Somehow, I had forgotten my second one! I'm still not sure why or how I missed that in my checklist; I can only

---

72 Technically speaking—this isn't the mountaineering "Death Zone"—that doesn't start for another 2,400 feet. But it was the highest I had ever been, and in the moment, I thought it might be the death of me, so please allow me a bit of poetic license.

describe it as one of those stupid mistakes I made because of a combination of haste and altitude-induced cognitive impairment.

Going back meant burning an hour of extra energy and falling behind the rest of my team, but climbing with only one liter of water would have been insane. I didn't really have any other choice but to retrace my steps and retrieve my second bottle of water.

When tragedy occurs, it's usually the result of a series of "cascading failures" where mistakes compound, and this was no different. Since I was an hour behind the rest of my group, I started pushing myself to climb faster to catch up. Some days, I was quicker than the other climbers and could have made the time up, but for whatever reason, I just didn't have my usual energy that day. And so, I began to get frustrated.

Since I was frustrated, I was moving less efficiently, which only made me more tired. And as I fell further behind, I took less time to rest. Since I was rushing through my rest breaks, I wasn't taking the time to eat or drink my water. I entered a vicious cycle where my frustration fed my bad decision-making, which in turn made me more tired and frustrated.

About eight hours into the climb, when I expected to have long been in camp, I was finally getting close. The safety of our tents seemed within reach, but the last section was particularly brutal. The ice was what climbers call "bulletproof"—sheer blue, slippery ice hard enough that my crampons could barely penetrate to get a toehold. My toe spikes kept slipping as I tried to ascend, exhausting me physically even as I got nowhere. Plus, it hurt like hell every time my feet slipped and my body banged into the ice wall.

Deep in this cycle of exhaustion, misery, and frustration, I tried to kick a toehold and my crampon slid crooked, dangling off my boot by just one strap. I wasn't carrying extra crampons in my pack. Even with *both* crampons attached, I was hardly making progress and exhausting myself. Without a crampon, I had no idea how I would get to Camp 3. Retreating to Camp 2 wasn't an option; it would have taken me hours to rappel back down. No way I would make it before nightfall. I'd be stuck in the no man's land in between camps, a nightmarish and life-threatening scenario.

For the first time in my climbing career, the idea of being stuck on the fixed line and freezing to death that night went through my mind. I wasn't ready to give up, but in that moment, I understood how climbers did and how they died of despair on the lines.

With some good luck and the grace of whatever gods watched over the mountain that day, I was able to hook my ice axe around

the crampon and delicately reattach it to my boot as I dangled from the rope. By this point, I was at the brink of exhaustion, and my nerves were shot. The fun was over, and I desperately wanted to quit.

I didn't think I had the energy to keep climbing, but I also knew I didn't have a choice. Realizing that my only choice was progress or freezing to death on the line, I kept moving one step at a time until I finally made it into camp. I took a picture of myself that evening before a horrible night of sleep, convinced that it was the highest I would ever be in my life. In that moment, my fear response completely consumed me, and I was certain I didn't have the strength to go higher. Looking back at that photo, my eyes are lifeless, and my cheeks are hollow. Everest looms behind me, so close and yet so far away.

TAKEAWAY FOR ENTREPRENEURSHIP

On the fateful climb from Camp 2 to Camp 3, I lost the ability to see clearly what was truly in front of me. I should have calmed down, stuck to my plan, and taken the day a step at a time. Instead, I rushed and almost ended up in a world of trouble.

JOURNAL PROMPT

How will you control the biases in your mind in order to see what is truly in front of you? How will you avoid being overwhelmed by enthusiasm or despair? What fears are lurking below that need to be evaluated clearly so that they will lose their power?

Forgiveness:
The Ability to Truly
Forgive Yourself

In my years spent studying mental resilience, the idea of self-forgiveness might be the most transformative lesson I have learned. It also might be the idea that feels the most subtle, the hardest to grasp and explain why it's so critical. The Entrepreneurial Advice Industry teaches us that hardened entrepreneurs are supposed to think about being tougher and grinding harder, not about forgiveness.

And yet, the concept of forgiveness is at the root of all lessons about resilience. If adaptability is the most important skill to survive and thrive in dynamic circumstances, forgiveness is the key to adaptability. Forgiveness teaches us to let go of the past and adapt to the present.

For years, I have mentored an entrepreneur I'll call Adam. Our discussions began with geeking out over technology patents on financial instruments and developed into a lifelong friendship built on weekly conversations. The purpose of these chats is for me to advise Adam, but I usually learn more than I teach.

We were a couple years into our conversations, and Adam's business was struggling. While the potential remained exciting, the market wasn't developing as quickly as he had expected, and he wasn't sure he had a viable financial pathway forward. He had put his life savings into the business and wanted desperately to grow it into the company he knew it could be.

Most entrepreneurs I know have some sort of contingency plan in the back of their minds to get by if their dreams don't come to fruition. I knew one CEO who moonlighted as an Uber driver. Personally, I always made sure that my personal expenses were low enough that I could support myself on tips as a bartender. Adam's contingency plan was to work at Home Depot, and he was about two weeks away from giving up the company and filling out an application.

As if that wasn't enough weight to carry, his wife had just told him she was leaving him. You can imagine the gut-wrenching agony Adam was going through in the moment. I can still feel my stomach tighten as I remember our conversation.

He had no doubt that he was still deeply in love with his wife, and he believed that she still loved him. As he tried to make sense of it, he relayed how she told him she had to go because of the toll the business was taking on their marriage. He interpreted this to mean he was a failure for not making enough money and providing enough cash flow into the relationship.

As we talked, it became apparent that she hadn't said any such thing! His Crocodile brain, manifesting shame and fear, was coloring how he interpreted her words. She was actually trying to get across a very different message: she hadn't signed up to be with someone who was miserable every day. Living with his misery, not their financial situation, was unsustainable to her. Whether rich or poor, she wasn't interested in living each day of her life in a joyless existence while her partner grew more miserable chasing the brass ring.

Adam considered himself a positive person, but as we talked through the situation, he realized he hadn't felt happy in years. We dug deep into the lack of joy in his life. That joylessness was rooted in previously unspoken shame of believing he was failing as a CEO. In his previous career as a commodities trader, he made great money and used that as a proxy to convince himself he was successful. But, he wasn't satisfied being a trader. He wanted to build, to create. And so, he answered his own call to adventure, left trading, and started a technology company.

Since the inception of the company, Adam had accomplished a lot! He had raised millions of dollars and built an amazing team and technology. The company was succeeding on a variety of metrics, except it hadn't nailed product/market fit and was not yet financially viable. He completely disregarded the fact that most transformative companies are in the same position for *years* after being founded. Based on the unrelenting standards he set for himself, Adam felt like a failure no matter what he accomplished. When we got to the root of the problem, Adam felt deeply ashamed of himself.

I'm using the word "shame" very deliberately to describe how Adam internalized the feeling of failure, the feeling that he wasn't doing his part despite all that he was accomplishing. To illustrate, here is a story from Brené Brown, the expert on feelings of shame:

> When Ellen was in kindergarten, her teacher called me at home one afternoon and said, "I totally get what you do now." When I asked her why, she said that earlier in the week, she had looked over at Ellen, who was in the "Glitter Center" and said, "Ellen! You're a mess." Apparently, Ellen got a very serious look on her face and said, "I may be making a mess, but I'm not a mess." (That's the day I became "that parent.") Charlie also gets the distinction between shame and guilt. When I found our dog pulling food out of the trash can, I scolded her by saying, "Bad girl!" Charlie came sliding around the corner, shouting, "Daisy is a good girl who made a bad choice! We love her! We just don't love her choices!" When I tried to explain the difference by saying, "Daisy is a dog, Charlie," his response was, "Oh, I see. Daisy is a good dog who made a bad choice." [73]

As with so many things, if we could simply absorb the wisdom of children, we would be much better off. Adam wasn't getting what Ellen and Charlie learned at a young age; he wasn't differentiating his humanity from his choices or those outcomes. Unfortunately, most of us adults have a voice of shame in our psyche constantly

73 Brown, Brené. *Daring Greatly: How the Courage to Be Vulnerable Transforms the Way We Live, Love, Parent, and Lead* (Garden City, New York: Avery Publishing Group, 2015). p. 225.

whispering in our ear. That voice tells us that we are lazy or weak because of our choices.

Forgiving ourselves is the art of soothing that negative voice, putting down the weight we are carrying, and relearning to feel joy in whatever circumstances we may find ourselves.

Adam wasn't just feeling some level of remorse for having made mistakes. What was going through his mind wasn't "I made some mistakes in the service of daring greatly." Instead, Adam had internalized the notion that he was personally a failure for the lack of immediate financial success and cash flow. And since he, like so many entrepreneurs, had essentially wrapped his personhood into his business, he felt like a personal failure.

I could relate. When I was at a similar stage of the journey, shame felt like the emotion I was *supposed* to feel. Given the need to succeed, the money at stake, and the strength I should be demonstrating, I wrongly assumed that the only reasonable emotion while the company is in financial distress is shame. Anything else might feel like I wasn't taking the situation seriously, like I was some sort of stupid, naïve, grinning idiot who didn't realize the challenge in front of me.

Adam agreed. What kind of a moron, we ask ourselves, could go home and be happy at the dinner table after yet another rough day at the office? We are *supposed* to be angry about our situation, dammit!

Adam allowed that shame to bleed into his soul and prevent him from being the partner he had committed to being for his wife. Despite his best efforts, he projected anger as a defense mechanism. He didn't talk with his wife about the objective reality of the company's situation. Instead of communicating, he stayed quiet and tried to shield her from the ups and downs he was experiencing, a misguided attempt at strength that only added to his burden.

Of course, Adam's wife understood far more of what was going on than he gave her credit for. She didn't want to be shielded from reality; she was happy to stand by his side while he fought those battles. She had signed up to support him during the ups and downs of the journey; she had *not* signed up to live in a perpetual state of joylessness and anxiety. She finally said "enough," not because the business was struggling, but because of his response to the shame of feeling like a failure.

The worst effects of the entrepreneurial journey come from our reaction to the struggle, not from the struggle itself.

Letting ourselves become overwhelmed with shame takes a challenging situation and makes it worse. Holding on to that shame robs us of our happiness, our joy, our ability to recognize beauty. Shame is the opposite of that most critical survival skill, adaptability. It is holding on to past events and mistakes rather than focusing our energy on evaluating what's to come and preparing for that.

Shame traps our psyche in a prison of punishing ourselves for past mistakes. It burdens our mind with the weight of those decisions, making our thinking less flexible. It erodes our self-confidence and thus our decision-making. It makes us less trusting of our senses, less able to see what is there, because we are constantly second guessing ourselves. Because we have made mistakes in the past, our internal monologue questions whether we are getting it right this time.

There is nothing more toxic in challenging situations than a leader silently wallowing in her own shame, clutching on to the thing that she desperately needs to release in order to be effective.

You will never be an effective leader while you remain trapped in your own prison of shame. Recognizing that voice, and then conquering it, makes you far more effective as a leader. Oh, and by the way, it makes you a much better partner and a much happier person!

Unfortunately, self-forgiveness is much harder than it sounds. The guilt, shame, and frustration take root deep within us. Below are four lessons to help.

Break the Event/Response Feedback Loop

At the time, raising my first round of capital was the hardest thing I had ever done. I considered myself someone who succeeded, and a lot of my ego was wrapped up in the fact that people generally were willing to bet on me. On some level, I knew that fundraising was hard and that most investors turn down most of the companies that pitch them. I understood that intellectually, but not emotionally.

Because of that, being rejected by a VC felt like a personal affront. If a VC wanted to negotiate on price or terms, I would understand. I could see a reasonable negotiation on the value. But the idea that most investors effectively valued my company at zero, evidenced by the fact that they were uninterested in investing, was something I had a really hard time processing. In my mind, the company was exceptional and I was someone to bet on. These facts were *so obvious* I couldn't understand how any investor wouldn't share my opinion.

Plus, there seemed to be this weird set of protocols and code words for VCs and successful CEOs that I didn't understand. I reached the conclusion that raising a seed round was as mysterious and irrational as trying to figure out how to sit with the cool kids in a middle school cafeteria.[74]

I remember a very distinct feeling that all of these rich people had all of this money, and the only person they weren't willing to fund was *me*.

It wasn't until I got to the other side of the table and started investing that I began to realize an investor's investment decision reveals more about them than the entrepreneur. Whether or not they invested in me had much more to do with their preconceived notions, general beliefs, age of fund, availability of additional capital, time, interest, and generally whatever was happening in their lives at that moment. Investors take a company, evaluate it against a set of oddly-defined pattern recognition algorithms, and come out with totally irrational answers! The best investors are self-aware enough to at least acknowledge that. But "it's not you, it's me" isn't really a satisfying rejection in any context, and certainly not to an entrepreneur.

Homework

To soothe that voice of negativity, cultivate a practice of self-gratitude. Wherever you are on the journey, you undoubtedly have more to be proud of than ashamed. When you hear that internal voice of negativity, reminding you of everything you have done wrong, stop what you're doing and take a breath or two. Name that voice (perhaps "Fred"). Write down the things that Fred is telling you to be ashamed of ("Another VC turned me down; I'm clearly no good at pitching investors").

---

74   Severinghaus, Erik. "NBC: Raising Seed Money: Lessons Learned from the Middle-School Cafeteria." Erik Severinghaus. https://www.severinghaus.com/new-blog/raising-seed-money-lessons-learned-from-the-middle-school-cafeteria.

Now, separate what actually happened ("A VC turned me down") from the story you are telling yourself ("I'm no good at pitching investors; I'm not worthy to be an entrepreneur").

Sit with that story. Is it factually correct? Is there contradictory evidence? Take the devil's advocate position and write down the contradictory evidence ("I know 99 percent of investor meetings end in a 'no,' so this is actually expected behavior. Plus, I had a good investor pitch last week").

Finally, remind yourself of three things that you're grateful for that have gotten you to this point. "I wouldn't even be in the room with these investors if our mutual contact hadn't thought enough of me to make an introduction. I wouldn't be worried about the investors helping me make payroll if I hadn't recruited such talented people to my team. I wouldn't even care about raising capital if I didn't have a product I was so excited about bringing to market."

If you can get in the habit of confronting the negative voice with a more rational and balanced perspective of what's actually happening, you'll find that the voice gets quieter and quieter over time.

Separate Your Humanity from Your Profession

As SimpleRelevance approached the brink of failure, I had a long conversation with Kevin Willer, one of my earliest investors. I confided my fears and finally vocalized the overwhelming feeling that I was a failure for the fact that I wouldn't even return the capital he invested in the company, much less generate the return on investment I had expected. He started to probe the idea that I was a failure by asking me some great questions:

"How do you feel about the technology you guys developed?" I was exceptionally proud of it, and I believed with all my heart that we had moved the field forward by developing a new and useful way of approaching artificial intelligence.

"Do you think your team regrets having joined the company?" I was confident that almost every person on the team had grown and developed, and I felt proud of the role they played in building the company.

"Do you think your customers regret working with you?" In fact, we had generated amazing returns for most of our customers. We found ways to create value for even the most difficult customers.

"Are you proud of how you conducted yourself?" I believed I had worked hard and conducted myself with integrity during the entire journey, doing everything I knew to move the company forward.

As he interrogated my shame, we agreed that the company and I had succeeded on many measures. Yes, we had failed to achieve the investor ROI we would have liked, and yes, that's an important metric to fail on, but it's not the *only* one. Failing on that metric doesn't make me a "failure." We so often forget to take credit for our accomplishments; instead, we punish ourselves mercilessly for our failures.

Homework

Using a journal, numerically rank how you feel about the following on a scale of 1–10:

- Your business
- Your family
- You as a person

Now explain why you put each of those numbers. What made that number better? What made it worse? Doing this consistently teaches us to interrogate our emotions and check in with our current emotional state, but it also helps separate the different aspects of ourselves. Give yourself permission to have a "self" score that's higher than your business score! It's okay to be happy with yourself as a person, even if your business struggles.

The trick to this is using your journal to remind yourself of what seems like an obvious truth but so often gets lost: you are not your company; you are so much more than your business.[75]

Write Your Anti-Biography

I have always had a sense that one of the VC firms that "gets it" is Bessemer Venture Partners. My perception isn't driven by their (exceptional) track record of venture investing or all the accolades they've received. I know lots of famous VCs that don't impress me.[76] My long-standing respect for them isn't because of their successes, but rather their thoughtful and public account of their failures. Their "Anti-Portfolio" website is an honest and hilarious recounting of why they chose not to invest in such "obvious failures" as Google or Netflix.[77]

Inspired by Bessemer, I sat down and wrote my anti-biography. I initially did it because I always felt like a bit of a fraud when I would send people my biography for speaking engagements. These bios are always full of accolades, designed to make me sound like a compelling person so that an audience will want to show up and hear me talk. While everything in the bio was true, I conveniently skipped over the hard times and the failures. For someone who rails against selection bias in the stories we tell entrepreneurs, writing a biogra-

---

75   Whenever I think about this, I am reminded of the Chuck Palahniuk quote from *Fight Club*: "You are not your job, you're not how much money you have in the bank. You are not the car you drive. You're not the contents of your wallet. You are not your fucking khakis."

76   Remember, luck is usually as important in this game as skill.

77   https://www.bvp.com/anti-portfolio/.

phy of myself that selects only my greatest accomplishments felt hypocritical. I was perpetuating the very pressure that I was fighting against! I didn't want to be just another person telling entrepreneurs, "be strong like me and everything will work out great."

And so, I decided to write my anti-biography, the other side of the story:

> Climbing Mount Everest was the second hardest thing I have ever done. The second nearest I have ever felt to dying.
>
> The first is being an entrepreneur.
>
> During my career, I've closed down six companies, losing over $2 million of investor capital in organizations as wide ranging as tech startups, consultancies, and even a board game business (the games from which I literally could not give away). I have been let go twice, including from a side job selling Cubs charity raffle tickets. I was once called "the single worst investment ever made" by a prominent Chicago investor. I have had investors renege on deal terms and give me fake wire transfer numbers while assuring me that the money I needed to avoid bankruptcy was on the way. I have watched trusted mentors rip off my business ideas and release them as their own. The entrepreneurial journey has cost me an engagement, a best friend, a six-figure bank account, and probably a few years of my life. Sometimes I can barely make it out of bed in the mornings thanks to a herniated disc in my back.
>
> These struggles have made me who I am and are the keys that unlocked my achievements.

It was one of the most cathartic things I have ever done. Giving light to my most embarrassing failures and weaknesses completely dissolved their power over me. In fact, it felt so good that I decided to post my anti-biography on my website for everyone to see! As the old saying goes, "Once you have ruined your reputation, you can live quite freely." When I'm introduced to an audience as some sort of a learned and gifted superman who turns everything he touches to gold, I no longer have to worry if anyone in the audience actually knows about all the mistakes I have made. I don't have a voice in my head telling me that if they only knew my full story, they would recognize me as an imposter. I know the audience is quite aware of my shortcomings—I have already told the world!

Homework

Write your anti-biography. It can be short or long, recent or comprehensive, but honestly document those things that you're ashamed of and the things that you hope people won't find out. Get those things out of your head and onto a piece of paper. Now, explain why you're thankful for those mistakes and weaknesses.

Decide what you'd like to do with that sheet of paper. There's nothing wrong with tearing it up, throwing it away, or burning it. If you're feeling particularly brave, review your anti-biography with people you love and trust. It's an amazing experience to own your failures, forgive yourself for them, and then be loved and accepted by others while they have full knowledge of your shortcomings.

The Power of No

One of the most powerful techniques I have learned is the art of respecting myself enough to say "no." Rather than trying to be all things to all people, I have learned to set boundaries for myself both personally and professionally. Learning the difficult art of saying "no" is an amazingly effective negotiating technique and an act of deep self-respect.

Many of us grow up learning "the customer is always right," and as an entrepreneur, I always felt like everyone was a customer! I was always selling to actual customers as well as investors, employees, and any number of other constituents. I sometimes even felt like my vendors were customers when I was trying to convince them to take a chance working with us. If the customer is always right, and everyone is a customer, that dynamic left very little space for the things *I* needed.

To make matters worse, I often wasn't saying "yes" from a place of authenticity. I would agree reluctantly, so my lack of boundaries would lead to resentment.

I thought of myself as a positive person. My general philosophy was to be from a place of "yes" and cultivate a mentality of abundance. [78] I still feel that way, but I've found the key to an effective "yes" is retaining the right to say "no." No, those payment terms don't work for me. No, that's not a party I want to go to. No, I'm not going to sacrifice my morning workout for an 8 a.m. meeting that isn't urgent.

By taking ownership of my own needs and feelings, I create authority and space for negotiation. I regain my own sense of agency and power in the conversation and feel more in control. I find that rather than being angry, others usually respect my answer and my willingness to be honest and authentic about how I'm responding to a particular request.

---

78   Adam Grant's *Give and Take* is a fantastic book on the importance of cultivating an abundance mentality.

Homework

List three requests people have made of you in the last few days that you accommodated with a "yes" but did so grudgingly. The ones that you didn't want to say "yes" to but felt like you "really had to." Now role-play with a journal or trusted partner what would have happened if you had said "no." How do you expect they would have responded? Would there have then been a negotiation at that point? How would you have felt if you asserted yourself in that moment and put your needs on at least equal footing with the needs of others?

The next time a request comes in that you don't feel good about accommodating, consider responding with "no, I won't, and here's why." Start with low-risk requests to develop the muscle, but learn to assert yourself in that moment where you are feeling stretched. You'll likely find it to be an amazingly freeing experience.

LESSON FROM MOUNT EVEREST

Throughout my years of adventure activities, I have had my fair share of brushes with mortality. I climbed down a wet cliff while lost one night on Kilimanjaro, almost slipping off and falling. I was once caught in an avalanche on Aconcagua. Another time I was trapped below a class five river rapid in West Virginia. I have seen too many body bags carried off mountains and had friends who died tragically in the outdoors.

I have come face to face with danger several times, but I have never wanted to quit. Sure, I've decided not to ski or climb certain slopes because the risk seems too high, but I have never been scared to the point of feeling like I need to quit altogether. That climb to Camp 3 was the first and only time I really felt that feeling in the mountains. The feeling that I didn't belong and shouldn't be there, the feeling that I really needed to quit.

After spending a rough night at Camp 3, we returned to the relative safety of Camp 2 the next day. When I finally had the time to think about it, I decided it was time to quit. Even if I didn't realize it, fear had taken over and was the dominant emotion driving my decision-making. I used my satellite phone to text my girlfriend back home to ask her to help me book a flight from Kathmandu. I was ready to be done, certain that the mountain had beaten me.

I had with me a small bag of keepsakes to take to the summit. There were some small gemstones and keychains I wanted to take to the top of the world, and a special Chicago Cubs flag signed by my friends and family at my going away party. I hated the feeling that I was letting everyone down who believed in me by not getting these objects to the summit.

My tent mate and best friend on the mountain, Brooke, saw the emotion on my face and made one of the kindest offers imaginable, telling me he would take my keepsakes to the top with him as I went home. At high altitude, each ounce of weight you carry feels like a pound, and there is a razor thin margin between climbing success and failure. Offering to carry extra weight for someone else is absolutely not a thing that anyone does. I was touched beyond words by his generosity.

As I sat, wallowing in my own little pity party, our guides Harry and Kevin came to the tent. I was sure they were going to tell me I wasn't good enough or strong enough to be climbing Everest.

I had already played out the conversation with them; I knew exactly how it would go. They would tell me they were sorry, but I had to go home for the safety of my teammates and myself. They would say that they knew I felt bad, but it just wasn't in the cards for this year.

I felt like a fraud who had no business being there in the first place. I felt like the mountain had exposed me as an imposter. As they entered the tent, I prepared myself so that I wouldn't break down and cry. At least I could try to handle my failure with dignity.

Like so many bouts of Imposter Syndrome, this one was only in my imagination. Instead of telling me I needed to leave the mountain, they came to reassure me. They told me the climb had been brutal, even for them. They reminded me about my slow start and having to go back to camp and retrieve my water bottle. Most importantly, they assured me that even though I struggled and felt unsafe, I performed reasonably well. Their confidence meant a lot to me.

Even more impactful than their expert assessment was their historical data. IMG tracked Everest climbers' times on each stage of every climb over the past ten years, and they showed me my times were aligned with other successful climbers. Although I had judged myself a failure, the data showed that I had pretty good odds of success.

And so, thanks to the help of Harry and Kevin, I got out of my own head. I was able to see my climb to Camp 3 as the successful completion of a hard day's work, not a failure to live up to some self-imposed standards. I mentally reframed that day as proof of my endurance and ability to overcome, not as a near catastrophe.

And then there was Dana, my girlfriend back home. I was texting her that I was ready to come home and asking her help to arrange a flight to get me out of there ASAP. Her response was amazing, and exactly what I needed in that moment. She began by assuring me that she would love me and be proud of me even if I quit the next day. From Dana's texts halfway around the world, I got the love, kindness, and support I needed to feel safe in that moment.

With that as the foundation, she gently prodded me to evaluate my own decision-making to be sure I wasn't making rash judgment during an emotional moment. She challenged me to consider if I was "really, really ready" to quit. She knew that the worst outcome would be to come home feeling like I hadn't given the climb everything I had. I wouldn't be able to forgive myself if I didn't give it my absolute best effort, and the vision of Everest would only stalk my dreams more vividly than it had for the past ten years.

I'll be forever grateful that Dana put aside her own self-interest, concerns for my safety, and a desire to have me home to focus on giving me the support I needed.

That combination of emotional support, context, and data restored my confidence and allowed my Philosopher brain to retake the upper hand from the Crocodile that was cowering in fear. The embarrassment of Imposter Syndrome went away, and I saw the challenge for what it actually was, not the story my fear response was telling me.

I forgave myself and recognized the accomplishment of making it to Camp 3 rather than punishing myself for not finishing the climb faster. Through that lens, I rebuilt my confidence and gained the strength to keep going. I decided that I had made it through that particular day, and I would keep making it through each day until I either quit or succeeded.

I'm trying hard to not make this sound corny or cliché, but the cold, hard reality of the situation was that I very nearly gave up on my dream of climbing Everest because I didn't believe in myself. The real shame is that I was prepared. I had the skills and the stamina. I had done the hard work to prepare myself and to ultimately succeed.

I very nearly gave up my dream because I was ready to listen to the part of my mind that is always convinced I'm not good enough.

TAKEAWAY FOR ENTREPRENEURSHIP

Forgiveness is a key for high performance. Until I was able to forgive myself for a less than stellar day, I wasn't able to adapt to the present and see the world clearly. Learning how to forgive yourself is a prerequisite for high achievement and happiness on the journey.

JOURNAL PROMPT

How often in your life do you feel contentment and joy? Are you standing in the way of your own ability to feel joy? Are you punishing yourself for perceived failures and shortcomings? If so, what are they? Is that punishment fair to yourself? How can you forgive yourself for the mistakes you have made so you can stop focusing on the past and instead live in the present while preparing for the future?

Stillness:
The Ability to Be Truly Still

*Who can (make) the muddy water (clear)? Let it be still, and it
will gradually become clear. Who can secure the condition of rest?
Let movement go on, and the condition of rest will gradually arise.*

—LAO TZU,
Tao Te Ching

The idea that more action, more motion, more *doing* is the solution to every entrepreneurial problem is deeply engrained in our collective psyche. We constantly hear that the winners of the entrepreneurial competition will be the ones who hustle harder, who outwork the competition.

Entrepreneur, author, and coach Jerry Colonna got stuck in this feedback loop of using activity as a proxy for happiness. In his book *Reboot*, he shares his personal story, using "lemon drops" as a metaphor for the happiness he was seeking:

> Looking back, I see all those subway rides, all that motion, as an attempt to gather lemon drops. My twisted logic went

like this: I didn't have any lemon drops, and therefore felt exhausted and depleted and constantly battled migraines, because I wasn't doing enough. The answer, therefore, was simple: Do more, faster.

As someone who is goal driven by nature and has a bit of a masochistic streak, "do more, faster" became an easy solution to every problem. Am I stressed? Do more, faster. Is the company struggling? Do more, faster. Current strategy not working? Don't stop and analyze, do more, faster.

I was living the famous Hunter S. Thompson quote, "Faster, faster, faster until the thrill of speed overcomes the fear of death." If I just kept going, I thought perhaps I could outrun my demons and doubts. In the back of my mind, I knew that the philosophy of constant acceleration had not ended well for the great gonzo journalist, but I avoided confronting that inconvenient realization as I lived his mantra.

There is a good reason that the idea of constant activity has taken such a strong hold in the entrepreneurial community. Entrepreneurship is an exercise in making things happen with imperfect information, a constantly shifting landscape, and the haze of ambiguity. If you put most corporate middle-managers in an entrepreneurial context, they become paralyzed by constant analysis, unable to execute on "good enough" because they need everything to be perfect. Entrepreneurs who allow themselves to sit around thinking and waiting for everything to be perfect would run out of money long before they got anything done.

But, advising entrepreneurs to do more activity is usually preaching to the converted; few of us need to be told that the clock is ticking and we are running out of money. Rarely does the person pre-wired for analysis paralysis decide to leave a safe job to pursue the challenges of startup land. Most of us want, as Teddy Roosevelt described it, to "get action." And so, entrepreneurial advice becomes a self-perpetuating loop of action-biased people telling each other to work harder if they want to succeed.

The simplicity of "work harder" allows the advice to spread like a rhetorical virus. It sounds like such a *tough* answer. And so, the message gets repeated and amplified in the entrepreneurial echo chamber until it loses all nuance and becomes the default answer to every question.

That dynamic was clear in my life. I vividly remember attending a CEO forum where my peer entrepreneurs asked me if I ever took time to relax. The closest thing I could think of to relaxation was the time I spent on long bike rides or runs, when at least I wasn't thinking about work. I could only quiet my mind through activity. The truth is that I had completely lost the ability to enjoy stillness. I had forgotten how to *just be.* I could no longer enjoy the company of others, or even be by myself, without the expectation for productivity or motion.

Because I lost the notion of stillness, the idea of a vacation on the beach sounded like hell to me. The idea of sitting. Of being still. Of being quiet and alone with my thoughts and feelings. Terrifying.

Besides, I knew I would want to work the whole time, and then I'd be frustrated that I was less effective than in the office. I think that's why I developed mountain climbing as a hobby. There is a tragic logic to the idea that I should go climb mountains if the only way to be present in the moment and avoid the anxiety of work was to be anchored by a very real threat of death.

And therein lies the problem of "do more, faster." As a mantra, it doesn't know nuance. It's a solution for nearly every problem.

There's no balance to it. It's so much less sexy to say "do more, faster, unless the things you are doing are potentially counterproductive to your success. In that case, you should slow down, prioritize, and ensure that you do the most important things well and ignore the rest." A sentence like that is never going to go viral! It's not a pithy answer to what ails you.

Pithiness aside, almost every over-achiever eventually comes to recognize that the balance between recovery and performance is critical to sustained success. Take Olympic athletes for example. On average, Olympians train thirty to forty hours a week. The best athletes in the world are preparing for the most competitive stage by "working" hours that most entrepreneurs would deride as "part time." And why is that? Is it because Olympians are lazy? Obviously not.

The reason Olympians have that sort of a work and rest ratio is because it's the most effective way to drive performance. The evidence is unequivocal.[79] Working more than fifty hours a week results in rapidly diminishing marginal returns—whether you're an entrepreneur or an athlete.

We describe being a "workaholic" in joking terms, but it's a real thing. At some point along the journey, many of us become addicted to the activity. We forget how to relax. We become so wrapped up in constant motion that the craving for activity itself becomes the goal, rather than a means to accomplish something. We become addicted to the act of working regardless of the productivity.

To be clear, there's nothing wrong with using that "extra gear" of exceptional effort many of us have developed to outwork our peers. That's a valuable tool when properly harnessed and used

---

79   Pencavel, John. "The Productivity of Working Hours." Stanford University. April 2014. http://ftp.iza.org/dp8129.pdf.

intentionally. But the activity must be balanced with recovery. True relaxation. Stillness. For many of us who get addicted to the activity, being comfortable in the quiet may be harder than physically demanding, grueling activity.

Training our mind to be comfortable with stillness for longer and longer periods of time is no different than training our bodies for a marathon, getting comfortable running for longer and longer periods of time.

Break the Interruption Addiction

I never kept track, but I'd be willing to bet that I checked my watch, phone, and computer more than one thousand times some days as an entrepreneur.[80] I convinced myself that knowledge is power and that my brain needed to be constantly processing a steady stream of inbound information. Plus, it made me feel important to always be connected. One of the many ways our brain gets hijacked by modernity is the squirt of dopamine we get every time something interrupts us. In the evolutionary sense, this is a useful adaptation since things that interrupt our attention were usually threats or food, something we should quickly pay attention to.

That tendency gets coopted when we spend hours in front of phones and computers that are designed and optimized to constantly interrupt our focus. Like most people, I had a computer, a phone, and a watch all set to constantly make noise and vibrate at news, social media, email, phone calls, text messages, and any other conceivable event. My attitude was "throw as much information at my brain as possible, and let it process everything." I convinced myself that I was the Michael Jordan of multi-tasking and

---

80 That's about once a minute for eighteen hours a day, which sounds about right.

was setting an amazing example for my team by always responding to everything immediately.

Reading Nassim Nicholas Taleb's *The Black Swan* changed my life on that front:

> I propose that if you want a simple step to a higher form of life, as distant from the animal as you can get, then you may have to denarrate, that is, shut down the television set, minimize time spent reading newspapers, ignore the blogs.[81]

Heresy! Reducing the flow of information into my mind flew in the face of every instinct I had. Until that point, I treated my brain like some sort of voracious predator that must always be fed. I decided to try a completely different experiment. Before I would consume information, I would consider whether it was worth my time and attention, and ask myself three questions:

- Is this information critical to some task that I need to perform? (An email from a co-worker providing context on something that's important for me to respond to instead of the endless emails that I'm copied on but don't need to act upon.)
- Is this something that will still be valuable and useful in a year's time? (Meditations by Marcus Aurelius becomes more valuable with time, whereas a newspaper article from today will probably be useless in a year.)
- Is this something I am reading for sheer pleasure? (A novel by Christopher Moore may have no utilitarian value, but I love the humor.)[82]

---

81 Taleb, Nassim Nicholas. *The Black Swan: Second Edition: The Impact of the Highly Improbable* (Incerto).

82 Like *Lamb*. Or *Coyote Blue*.

If the information falls into one of those three categories, I'm all for it! Ninety percent of the news, social links, tweets, Facebook messages, and other things that constantly interrupted my thinking fell outside those filters, and I now safely ignore them. Information must first pass a filter of "why is this worthy of my attention" before I'm willing to ingest it.

The change is transformative: I find that I have much more time for the things I value and am distracted far less by things that are a waste.

In doing so, I have set either an explicit or implicit responsiveness expectation with people who message me. Everyone who knows me knows that I respond to text messages or phone calls/voicemails as soon as possible.[83] I respond to email occasionally, and I will check other messages (Slack, LinkedIn, Facebook, Google Chat, Twitter) on the rare occasion that I happen to be bored.

This is yet another lesson I have learned from my friend, Charlie. Charlie is the kindest and most thoughtful person I know; there is no one more committed to being a good friend than he is. If you call him, you know with absolute certainty that he'll call you back as soon as he can, probably after a few beers at 2 a.m. his time. On the other hand, if you email Charlie, there's about a 25 percent chance he'll respond, and that response may be delayed by a month or more. If one of my other friends didn't respond to multiple emails, I'd reasonably assume they are angry and ignoring me. With Charlie, I just know he doesn't respond to email…. I don't hold it against him! I simply call him instead.

As I thought about why I don't get upset when Charlie doesn't respond to me, I realized that we all influence the expectations that

---

83   Like most of the advice in this book, I feel compelled to make explicit that I'm not perfect. But I at least try to hold myself accountable to responding to these in a timely fashion.

come from others. If we allow ourselves to become slaves to the idea that we must always respond to the endless stream of inbound requests, we have no time to live life on our own terms. So long as our intention is pure, we just need to be willing to free ourselves of the expectations of others. Do the right thing with a pure heart, and others will adjust their expectations accordingly.

Homework

Decide on the one or two communications channels that you'll be highly responsive to. This might be Slack, email, or phone calls, but make it *no more* than two channels. I like phone calls and text messages because it imposes the highest cost on whoever is trying to reach me, which improves the signal-to-noise ratio. Let everyone who is important to you know that you will be highly responsive on those channels, but reserve the right to be slow on any others. We live in a world of semi-synchronous communication, and one of the keys to reducing the innumerable messages we all have and haven't responded to is to simply set the expectation of which queue is synchronous (will be prioritized and responded to) and which is asynchronous (will be responded to in due time…probably…unless the queue becomes overwhelmed).

Similarly, prioritize between zero and one source of news that you must know in real time. I find that I don't actually need any news interruptions in my day, and I'm still pretty well aware of what's happening in the world, so I'd suggest that the number of news alerts we really *need* might be zero, but I'll understand if you need to start with one.

Now, take a ruthless knife to eliminating every other interruption of your attention. Every other social channel, news channel, communication channel, photo alert, etc. Decide that you will check and respond to them on your own terms and resolve not to carry the unreasonable expectation of others on your shoulders. Ignore that feeling of fear of missing out, and it will eventually go away.[84]

Incorporate Digital Detox Breaks

Even as I reduced the interruptions, my phone remained a force for distraction, subtly reminding my brain to always be processing and thinking about the stressors in my life. Reducing the interruptions helped manage that anxiety, but I found I needed even deeper rest at times. There is something about simply having my phone and knowing that it could ring at any moment, interrupting whatever I'm doing and forcing me back into the problems of the world, that exacts a small but constant drain on my energy.

Realizing this, I resolved to give myself complete breaks from my phone. My ego fought tooth and nail against the idea that this might be possible. How would the world keep turning if I wasn't a connected part of it? Could my ego handle the possibility that I might not be so damn important that I wouldn't even be missed if I was out of touch for a bit?

I started to give myself digital connectivity breaks by using the time I spent on airplanes. I decided to not fight the battle of crappy airplane Wi-Fi and chose to stay out of touch on flights. I almost completely stopped connecting while on airplanes, and I used that time to read, write, nap, or anything else I could do on a plane but off the internet.

---

84   I have only made one exception to this rule in the past four years. A friend gave me a prototype for a mindfulness wristband that vibrates at random intervals throughout the day. The purpose of it is to interrupt my day and remind me to breathe and be present, if only for a moment. These mini-breaks have become interruptions in my day that I really look forward to.

Next, I changed my sleep routine. I installed a landline telephone and sent the number to my friends and family so they could reach me in case of emergency. Feeling absolved of guilt, I began to turn my cell phone off before bed. Pretty soon, I started turning it off an hour or two before bed, just to give myself time to decompress without worrying it would buzz. Same thing in the morning; instead of waking up and assuming that I must immediately connect, I try to go an hour with my family or myself before I connect my mind to the needs of the world. In addition to morning and evening, I now spend an hour either going for a walk or having dinner with my family with my phone completely off.

After these changes, I am able to see my phone for what it truly is—a machine to tie me to a world of expectations set by others. It's a useful device, but one that drains my attention and energy while tricking me into thinking that it makes me happy. Building these digital detox breaks helps me have far more energy, recover more effectively, and reduce my stress over the course of the day.

Homework

Once you have reduced the interruptions, start incorporating mental breaks for recovery during the day. The goal is to allow your mind to rest by removing the interruptions that exhaust it. First, focus on the time immediately before and after sleep. Sleep is obviously critical to the recovery process, and the more you can allow your body to ease in and out of sleep, the more productive that recovery will be. Start with a simple challenge: can you go five minutes without your phone before you go to bed? Ten minutes? Twenty? Thirty? Sixty? Can you use that time to read a book, journal, or meditate?

Maybe talk with a loved one? Generally, do anything that relaxes your mind, rather than stimulating it.

The same thing goes for waking up in the morning. Can you expand the number of minutes between waking up and facing the pressures of the day? Try to consistently go forty-five minutes in the morning without looking at your phone.

Finally, incorporate a break during the day to physically turn off your phone. Whether you go for a walk or eat dinner with your family, hold yourself accountable to at least an hour a day where your phone is completely inaccessible. Engage with the world and force yourself to be present.

Doing this felt extremely uncomfortable at first. My ego would scream at me that I was too important to be without my phone for those few minutes. If I allowed my body to indulge in a few hours of sleep, it would be selfish to my teammates to not immediately engage with whatever was waiting for me when I woke up. It seemed lazy, like I was setting a bad example for my team that I wasn't committed.

Upon reflection, these were all excuses and rationalizations I used to convince myself to avoid stillness, and *those excuses* set the bad example for my team. I should have been modeling resilience rather than compulsive activity. Building in digital detox breaks will help you be far more focused, energized, and balanced during the times that you are intentionally tuned in and working.

Reduce Unnecessary Stimulants

When you break the addictive cycle of interruption and activity and learn to incorporate stillness, you will find that your mind begins to operate much more efficiently. You perform better when called upon and recover better in the rest periods. Your sleep patterns will improve and you'll need fewer outside stimulants to deliver the same level of performance.

For most of my life, I lived on a steady diet of more than two liters of Coca-Cola a day plus a few Red Bulls thrown in for good measure. A steady stream of caffeine and sugar became my magic elixir, keeping me functioning at what I thought was my highest level for days on end. To top off the stimulants cocktail, I might pop an Adderall to fight off a hangover and keep me going after a long night. Remember, my answer to every challenge was "more activity," and the only way for me to continue to add to my activity load was through more stimulants. This is the natural result of an obsessive need to "do more, faster."

My personal story with stimulants doesn't have a dramatic ending; I don't have my own version of the classic *Saved by the Bell* scene of Jessie Spano singing "I'm So Excited" until I breakdown.[85] My demons have never primarily been with substances. But that isn't true for everyone, and it doesn't mean that constantly flooding myself with stimulants didn't take its toll on my mind and body.

I found that incorporating stillness, rest, and quiet allowed me to have better recovery. This, in turn, gave me the energy to lean less on the crutches of chemical energy. As I phased stimulants out, it allowed for even deeper rest, reinforcing a virtuous cycle of feeling better, resting better, and performing better.

I'm still not a teetotaler; I love a hot cup of coffee and don't personally fall in the camp of "remove all caffeine or stimulants." That's just not my personal vibe—the important part is to be intentional about the stimulants you do use.

---

85   dan182. "Jessie Spano Caffeine Pill Freakout!" YouTube. https://www.youtube.com/watch?v=bflYjF90t7c.

Homework

Be thoughtful about the stimulants you're putting in your body. Especially consider caffeine, refined sugars, carbohydrates, and amphetamines. Journal how you feel hourly for the course of a week to see if some of the highs from stimulants are causing crashes as well. As you add stillness into your day and week, does that improve your ability to rest and recover? In doing so, can you begin to wean yourself off stimulants and perhaps reinforce the system of allowing your body natural recovery rather than using the stimulants to override your natural rhythms?

Meditate

> When one gives undivided attention to the (vital) breath, and brings it to the utmost degree of pliancy, he can become as a (tender) babe. When he has cleansed away the most mysterious sights (of his imagination), he can become without a flaw.
>
> —Tao Te Ching

The path to being calmer, more centered, less reactionary, and more thoughtful becomes clear when you are able to take even a few minutes to concentrate on your breathing, your being, and quiet the voices in your mind (what Tao Te Ching describes as the imagination).

Like forgiveness, for a long time, I dismissed meditation as "hippie shit." What could possibly be learned by sitting on a floor, chanting, breathing, or whatever? That seemed like the opposite of learning, developing, and executing. In fact, the idea of meditating as an entrepreneur struck me as inane to the point of being comical. It was a farce manifested by those weirdos in California.

The only reason I ever got around to trying meditation was that it was suggested it to me by high achieving corporate types. I was at a bachelor party with a group of five senior executives and successful entrepreneurs. These high achievers agreed that the most important app they had ever downloaded was called Headspace, which led the user through a guided meditation for ten minutes a day. I decided to give it a try—even if I wasn't yet convinced.

I downloaded Headspace and used it sporadically for the first few months, maybe once or twice a week. I got no noticeable benefit from it whatsoever. Eventually, I followed through on my commitment to consistently use the tool, meditating five or six times a week for ten minutes per session. After a month, I felt myself transformed and became a believer.

Once I began consistently meditating, I found myself better able to control my thoughts, emotions, and reactions. It helped me recognize, acknowledge, and ultimately address cravings and desires that led to destructive behaviors. Meditation helps me concentrate, sleep, think, respond, and write far more effectively. In so many ways, it feels like a magical performance-enhancing drug without the side effects of pharmaceuticals.

My anecdotes and experiences with meditation are consistent with the literature. Meditation is consistently shown to reduce stress, reduce anxiety, improve concentration, and increase awareness. By virtue of these things, meditation also tends to kick-start a virtuous cycle, encouraging other healthy behaviors like exercise and nutrition.

Homework

Getting started with meditation is straightforward, and most people see noticeable gains in mental clarity after consistent practice of less than a month. Popular phone apps to encourage meditation include

Headspace[86] and Calm.[87] Mindfulness Coach[88] is a free app from the Department of Veterans Affairs. There are retreats, meditation centers, and all sorts of other ways to begin down the path. As with many things, initial consistency is the key to making the change. Ten minutes a day, six days a week for a month should be your minimum initial commitment. After that you can re-evaluate and decide whether to spend more time, maintain that cadence, or ultimately if it's not for you.

LESSON FROM MOUNT EVEREST

I started this book with the idea that entrepreneurship and mountaineering are similar at the most basic level. To succeed, you need to stay alive, not quit, and keep walking uphill. So long as you do that, you'll eventually achieve the goal. That's actually not quite accurate in either mountaineering or entrepreneurship, because the mantra assumes continuous progress without ever needing to retreat. In fact, both mountaineering and entrepreneurship require what feels like way too much time backtracking.

One of the more puzzling components of mountaineering to an observer is how much time and energy you spend going down the mountain instead of up. As your body goes further above sea level, there is less oxygen in the air. The air at Everest Base Camp (17,750 feet), contains about half the oxygen as the air at sea level. The higher you go, the lower the oxygen saturation. As the air you breathe becomes thinner, your body adjusts with adaptive mechanisms like manufacturing more red blood cells. If your body doesn't

---

86   https://www.headspace.com/.
87   https://www.calm.com/.
88   https://mobile.va.gov/app/mindfulness-coach.

adapt appropriately, it can lead to diseases like High Altitude Cerebral Edema (swelling of the brain) or High Altitude Pulmonary Edema (swelling of blood vessels around the heart). Both of these conditions are serious and can be fatal.

To counteract the effects of altitude on the body, mountaineers climb high into the altitude, rest for several hours (or even overnight) and then descend to recover. Making progress up the mountain requires a constant cycle of climbing higher to break through to a new threshold, adapting, and then heading back down to safety to rest. If you continue pushing forward without the recovery, even the strongest climber will succumb to the stresses lack of oxygen puts on the lungs, heart, and brain.

My first three climbs up Everest were only practice climbs. They got me comfortable on the mountain, allowed my body to adapt, and prepared me for the final push to the summit. Ironically, many climbers go way down the mountain before going to the top. Before pushing to the summit, they may go all the way down to about 11,000 feet to the largest village in the region, known as Namche Bazaar. Namche has restaurants, reasonably reliable internet, and is home to the world's highest bar.[89] While spartan compared to the comforts of the first world, life in Namche is luxurious compared to being on Everest.

And so, before the final push, I walked for two days to Namche. Bad weather was coming in, and we knew it would be at least a week before we could begin the climb. We were all given a choice: either ride out the storm at Base Camp or head to Namche (by foot or helicopter). About half of us chose Namche and half chose to stay at Everest Base Camp.

---

89   If you find yourself in Namche Bazaar, be sure to check out The Irish Pub. It's a phenomenal watering hole owned and run by the very friendly Dawa Sherpa.

That week in Namche was seven days of maddening stillness. At first, the luxuries were amazing. Televised sports, Maker's Mark whiskey, and hot fudge sundaes. But I wasn't in Nepal to revel in luxury. I was there to climb the mountain and was desperate to get on with it as soon as conditions would allow. Every day we would get up, check the weather, check in with Base Camp, and then kill another day just hanging out. Even worse, other teams were moving into position for their summit attempt while we cooled our heels in Namche, further stoking my fear of missing out.

At the time, it was frustrating as hell, but that stillness, quiet, and recovery proved critical to my ability to make it up the mountain. While in Namche, my stomach recovered, my muscles calmed down, and everything felt so much better. A few days of health and recovery, while frustrating in the moment, gave me the strength and energy I needed for the hard days to come.

TAKEAWAY FOR ENTREPRENEURSHIP

Like mountaineering, in entrepreneurship you have to go down in order to go up. Rest, recovery, and clarity of mind all come through stillness, which allows you to make the important pushes in a place much better equipped to succeed.

JOURNAL PROMPT

How often do you experience stillness in a given day or week? How often are you without action, activity, distraction, or busyness? How much time are you able to spend alone with your thoughts? Is that the right amount? Or is there an opportunity to be intentional to spend more time in contemplative stillness?

Presence:
The Ability to Be Truly
Present in the Journey

They form their purposes with a view to the distant future; yet postponement is the greatest waste of life; it deprives them of each day as it comes, it snatches from them the present by promising something hereafter. The greatest hindrance to living is expectancy, which depends upon the morrow and wastes today.

—SENECA,
On the Shortness of Life

The cruelest irony of being an entrepreneur may be that our anxiety about the present causes us to fixate on the future, robbing us of the joy we should experience during this adventure. We forget that we are living our dream!

Every entrepreneur I know, whether they exit for millions or for zero, looks back at the days of a small team solving exciting problems as the most fun of their professional careers. There is a *real-*

ness and authenticity to those moments that can never be replicated. The journey of the entrepreneur is an almost mystical transformative experience like nothing else in the world. There is something different about entrepreneurs, a *je ne sais quoi,* that is developed in the struggle and challenge.

How tragic then, that in the midst of the journey, we rarely appreciate it. I spent so much time fantasizing and looking ahead to the future that I wasn't in the moment. I became so fixated on the pain and the struggle that I lost all appreciation for the beauty of what I was able to get up and do every day.

Sacrificing the present to fixate on the future is sad in the existential sense that our life is a sacred gift to be enjoyed, but it's also counterproductive in a practical sense. Research shows that the mindset of looking ahead reduces our ability to process information in the present and overcome the challenges of the day. This doesn't mean we shouldn't consider the future and prepare for it— remember that the ability to prepare is one of the critical skills for success! This may sound a bit nuanced, but what it means is that when we are preparing, we should be present in that activity and focused on our preparation. When we are executing, we should be focused on that.

Let me explain what I mean. When I ran my first marathon, my previous longest run had been sixteen miles (and I had hurt myself going that far). The idea of running 26.2 miles filled me with anxiety. I wasn't sure I could do it—that's ten extra miles! The only way for me to think about the race was to ignore the fact that it was 26.2 miles. Instead, I thought about needing to run one mile, and I had to do that twenty-six times. I had already proven I could run one mile sixteen times, so why wouldn't I be able to do it twenty-six times? I also decided I would stop for a moment and celebrate at *each and every* aid station, which happened to be spaced one mile apart. I felt really dumb stopping at the aid station of the first mile, even if it was for just a quick moment of celebration. As I got to the dreaded mile markers beyond sixteen, I kept reminding myself that I only had to stay present in the moment, not think about the race, but just think about running to my next mile celebration.

And Everest. Well, that was a whole different beast. Looking up at that mountain filled me with both excitement and dread. I'd be overwhelmed if I thought about climbing the whole mountain. All I could focus on was each distinct day of the journey.

Entrepreneurship is no different. Although we prepare for what is to come, trying to discern the complete path from the present moment to the end of the journey is a fool's errand. When we allow ourselves to get caught up in the fear and frustration of how we solve for all of the problems in front of us, we lose the ability to enjoy and celebrate the amazing moments we experience each day. We miss the development of our junior staffers. We diminish the truth that our creation is generating value for our customers. Each day of the adventure has so many cool and amazing milestones if we can only be present to appreciate them.

Doing that makes us happier and more content. It reduces the odds that we will burn out. But it also increases our ability to process information and see what's around us. When we develop tunnel vision looking at the future, we miss the blindingly obvious facts in our midst. Being present makes us more emotionally receptive to our employees, better able to evaluate and coach them. It makes us less paranoid, more personable. More likely to be able to inspire others to follow us.

In both mountain climbing and entrepreneurship, I would oftentimes fantasize about fast forwarding to some future time when I was no longer putting in the work but enjoying the fruits of my success. Looking back, I realize how sacrilegious those fantasies are. I was wishing to forfeit precious days of my short life for the hope of some future fulfillment. While totally understandable to lighten my psychological load, this is a terrible trade! The joy is in the process.

How to Develop Reminders to Stay Present

Staying present isn't just an empty mantra, it's an ongoing challenge. I constantly find myself wanting to relitigate the past or anxiously live in the future, so I try to find ways to remind myself to stay grounded. Joseph Campbell writes a lot about the helpers and gifts that aid us as we go off on the hero's journey:[90]

> Once having traversed the threshold, the hero moves in a dream landscape of curiously fluid, ambiguous forms, where he must survive a succession of trials. This is a favorite phase of the myth-adventure. It has produced a world literature of miraculous tests and ordeals. The hero is covertly aided by the advice, amulets, and secret agents of the supernatural helper whom he met before his entrance into this region.

In my ongoing quest to stay present, I keep an amulet given to me by one of those supernatural helpers. Despite not being what I would describe as a jewelry guy, I wear a wristband that says "No Bad Days" given to me by my friend and inspiration, Ray Johnston. A

---

90 Campbell, Joseph. *The Hero with a Thousand Faces*. Princeton (N.J.): Princeton University Press, 1968.

talented point guard, Ray walked onto his college team at Alabama where he scored precisely zero baskets in his college career. After college, he outworked his peers to get a look from the Dallas Mavericks scouts. He was on the cusp of achieving his life-long goal, playing point guard for the Dallas Mavericks, when he discovered he had leukemia and would spend two and a half months in a medically-induced coma to recover.

With the damage to his lungs, toes that had to be amputated, and other scars from the surgery, Ray would never again come close to being the NBA athlete of his prime (although he has become one hell of a volleyball player). Rather than succumbing to the disappointment that could overwhelm anyone in that circumstance, Ray reinvented himself as a singer-songwriter, reminding his audiences that so long as they are alive, there are no bad days. Even the most challenging circumstances are a gift, compared to the alternative.

Being present in the moment is one of those things that's so easy to say and so hard to *do*. I can repeat my daily mantra of be present in the moment, re-read *The Power of Now*, and remind myself with my "No Bad Days" wristband, but I still find myself getting stuck in the future or the past. On Everest, my friend Charlie essentially anointed himself as my accountability buddy for being present in the journey. He kept me grounded by constantly reminding me to take the climb a day at a time and not to get lost in the fantasy of being home, that the things I longed for would be there when I did come home.

Since I have been home, my wife and daughter have become those people to me. My wife constantly reminds me that I am loved and accepted, and to be happy in the moment. She comes by that mindset naturally, and just being in her presence allows me to absorb it by osmosis. Similarly, my daughter's laugh has an almost supernatural ability to snap me out of whatever anxiety loop I find myself in—it's simply impossible for me not to be present when I'm looking at her smile or listening to her giggle.

I need all of these reminders to keep myself grounded and present. Morning and night, I remind myself, "See what is there, hear what is said, do the thing I'm doing, smooth away the ego, and accept change as it comes." Whenever I look at my wristband, I take a breath and remind myself to be present. When I really need to be brought back to the moment, I seek out Dana and Caroline, confident that they'll remind me why every moment we have is too precious to be squandered by anxiety about the future.

Homework

Develop a system of reminders to stay present in the moment. Whether it's physical reminders like a wristband or piece of jewelry or human beings who remind you to stay grounded, intentionally develop specific anchor points to remind yourself to take a breath and just enjoy the moment you're in without worrying about the future or the past. Ask someone in your life whom you trust to bring you back to the moment when they see you too far out of it.

168 Hours

The one thing we all have in common is that we have 168 hours of life in a week. One of the most important things we can do throughout our life is to be intentional about how we use those hours.[91]

---

91   The inspiration for this line of thinking initially came from Harry Kraemer and his excellent book, *From Values to Action: The Four Principles of Values-Based Leadership.*

By losing track of the present moment, I found that days, weeks, or months would get away from me. I felt reactive, almost like a boxer up against the ropes getting knocked around by the day-to-day life that I was living. I had a hard time keeping up with the constant inflow of tasks and information coming into my life. I always had more work to do, and I wasn't intentional about when to rest, when to work, and how to keep the rest of my life in balance.

During the most challenging times at SimpleRelevance, I would often go into the office over the weekend. It felt like the right thing to do for so many reasons—I could tell my friends and family I was "in the office." It made me feel like I was working hard and putting everything I had into the company. I always had the best of intentions about how much work I'd get done, how I'd get my to-do list clear and my inbox to zero, setting me up for an even more productive week. Plus, it'd be even more of an inspiration to my employees; they would know that The Boss was busting his butt to be in the office and working.

My dirty secret was that despite my best intentions, I often arrived on Saturday so exhausted from the week that I accomplished almost nothing, sometimes staring at my computer screen blankly. I'd try to get some busy work done and devolve to watching "just one TV show" on my laptop followed by "just one more." Anyone who has binge-watched TV shows will recognize exactly how much work I got done those days.

I was so exhausted and stressed that I could drag myself to the office but couldn't get my brain to functionally get work done. Worse, I'd beat myself up for my lack of productivity on Saturday and repeat the silly ritual on Sunday. By Monday, I would already be burnt out and in a worse position, not a better one. My lack of preparedness for my situation destroyed my ability to be productive, no matter how hard I tried.

Homework

What are the most important ways to think about your time? Write them down. You may have your own categories, but some typical ones are working, sleeping, family, friends, exercise. How many hours would you ideally spend in a typical week on these different activities?

Now look at your calendar from a "typical" week (I get that you're an entrepreneur, so no week is typical, but stay with me here). Last week if possible, but if last week was a weird one, then take another recent one. Do some quick analytics on your week. How many hours did you spend working? How many did you sleep? How many did you spend with family? Friends? Working out? Write down the number of hours in each category.

What's the delta between your ideal state and your actual state? How can you adjust your reality to move you closer to your ideal week?

Recognize When You're on Tilt

One of the first lessons you learn when playing poker is not to play "on tilt." The dynamic is a common one: you lose a bad hand or get bluffed, and it makes you angry. The adrenaline starts to pump, the vision narrows, and you're determined to "get back what is yours." Reason goes out the window, emotion takes hold. The Crocodile, not known for his poker skills, overrides the Philosopher. Getting your opponent to play while on tilt is one of the surest ways to take advantage of them, and playing while on tilt yourself is the quickest path to ruin.

At its heart, playing while on tilt is living in the past. It's getting stuck in the feedback loop of past hands and making poor decisions in the present because of that frustration. It leads to bad decisions and bad outcomes. In the entrepreneurial community, we do the same thing. We come in to work exhausted, frustrated by losing a customer, employee, or investor. We decide to double down, work harder, make more decisions. It's usually the wrong response, and we just make things more difficult on ourselves.

The key is to recognize when you're on tilt. Breathe. Sit a couple hands out. Go for a walk. Forget the past. Reorient yourself in the present moment. Once you have control of your emotions and are back in the present instead of emotionally living in the past hand, you can start playing again in full control.

Homework

Remember the last three times you were "on tilt." How did your head feel? Your shoulders? Your heart? Your chest? Your breath? What are the physical symptoms that tick up and signal that your mind is shutting down? Journal these symptoms to become more aware of them. As you go through your daily life, when you feel that "tilt" start to creep up, take a deep breath and remind yourself to calm down. If possible, take a break, take a walk, call a friend, or do other things to remove yourself from anything involving decision-making until you feel those symptoms of tilt recede and you're once again able to make a decision from a place of calm and balance.

Identify What's Being Left Unsaid

While I was struggling through The Death Zone of Imposter Syndrome, I wrapped myself in activity to avoid prioritizing the most important things in the present moment. If I was always looking ahead or deconstructing the past, I could avoid the reality of what was happening in the present. Looking back, I was avoiding burning questions that I wish I had the guts to ask and get the issues on the table rather than leaving them unsaid.

I wish I had asked a certain employee whether the contracts he was bringing me were fraudulent when I had my doubts.

I wish I had asked the employees I felt might be struggling whether the boss I had hired over them was properly supporting them.

I wish I had asked potential acquirers if there was a deal to be done earlier.

I have talked a lot in this book about using the Philosopher brain to override the Crocodile. In these and other instances, my Crocodile brain was screaming at me that something was wrong! He was gnashing teeth, causing stress, and generally trying to get my attention onto crucial issues I was leaving unresolved.

My Philosopher brain ignored and obfuscated all of this. I didn't want to face reality, so I left lots of conversations lurking below the surface. When I finally did surface these issues in many cases, it was too late to effectively course correct and mitigate the damage.

Homework

What is being left unsaid? What questions are being unasked? What conversation needs to be had that is being avoided? Sit with your journal or trusted advisor and discuss the most important questions.

LESSON FROM MOUNT EVEREST

Returning to Everest Base Camp from my long rest down in Namche, it was finally time for the summit push! Leaving Base Camp for the final climb, I felt like a kid on Christmas morning—if you were expecting Christmas time to be the hardest few days of your life. Even with that expectation in mind, I had no idea just how bad things were going to get.

Day one of the final climb was a climb straight to Camp 2 from Base Camp. Until that trip, we had always climbed to Camp 1, spent the night, and then gone to Camp 2. Camp 1 was barren and poorly apportioned, whereas Camp 2 was known as "Advanced Base Camp" with much better places to put tents, a proper dining tent, and even a Sherpa cook stationed there. Perhaps more importantly, we got to poop in the dignity of an actual toilet tent rather than in a bucket on the glacier in view of the world. We all felt pretty good as we made our way efficiently through the dangerous ice fall and got to Camp 1 right as the sun was coming up. I had started the day with two liters of water and was about halfway through as I paused for a short rest at Camp 1.

After a fifteen-minute rest, I decided to press on. The climb from Camp 1 to Camp 2 usually took me about four hours, and I figured with my fitness and acclimatization, I would make it in record time. I set out confident and excited, not thinking about the fact that every time I previously made the Camp 1 to Camp 2 climb had been before sunrise.

As the sun came up, the Western Cwm[92] became an oven. The high-altitude sun radiated off the snow and ice around me, and I very quickly started to feel the dizziness of heat exhaustion. Realizing I

---

92   The steep sided hollow path that connects Camp 1 to Camp 2.

only had one liter of water left, I became very conservative with how much I was drinking, making my dehydration worse. I was stuck in a vicious cycle where my exhaustion caused me to climb more slowly, which left me more exposed as temperatures rose, causing me to drink less water and become more exhausted. I was sick, nauseous, barely moving, and generally in a terrible situation. So much for my happy, easy climb to Camp 2!

Around me, other climbers were collapsing, barely moving, throwing up, and overcome with dehydration. It looked like a scene from a war movie with climbers collapsing all around me. I'm not sure I would have made it were it not for Pega, one of our trusty Sherpas, hauling a giant container of juice down from Camp 2 to rehydrate us and give us electrolytes and energy.

As I finally dragged myself into Camp 2, you can imagine how excited I was to lay down and rest. We had previously cached a lot of gear at Camp 2 in preparation for our final climb, and I could almost taste the king-sized Snickers bar I knew was in my bag waiting for me as a reward for making it.

And then, perhaps the most surreal thing to happen to me on the trip—that gear bag I had cached was nowhere to be found. Sherpas looked through tents and searched everywhere. We radioed other camps thinking that perhaps it had somehow been confused with someone else's gear, all to no avail. Somehow, my Camp 2 bag had vanished! I was exhausted, dehydrated, miserable, sad, furious.

Looking back, I can only describe my emotional state as being near tears that I wouldn't continue my climb, yet secretly relieved somewhere deep down that the ordeal would finally be over. It was so surreal to have no idea where my gear was. I was so beat. It felt like this might have been the universe telling me, "Enough!"

I spent that night in a sleeping bag one of the Sherpas was kind enough to loan me and woke up the next day to figure out a plan.

The guides offered to cobble together a serviceable summit gear kit from various people's extra supplies, but summiting Everest was intimidating even with everything going properly. I didn't like the idea of being in The Death Zone without my trusty equipment, and this just felt like a bad omen.

I was mercifully spared the decision of whether to throw in the towel by the sound of Sherpas celebrating and yelling at me to "come quick." My gear had been found!

Somehow, my bag managed to fall perfectly *between* the two fabric walls of our double-walled dining tent, completely out of sight. It was pure luck that one of the Sherpas thought to look in such an obscure spot.

The Sherpas finding the gear robbed me of my excuse for quitting, but I was still physically exhausted, stressed, emotionally drained, and just getting ready to start the hard work. Sitting in the same tent where I had almost quit the last time around (after my frustrating Camp 3 climb), I had to reestablish the same emotional strength. I meditated for a while and reminded myself I didn't need to climb the entire mountain—I only had to climb to Camp 3 the next day. I had already done it once, no reason to believe I couldn't do it again and better this time around. Don't fixate on the future, take it one day at a time.

The heat exhaustion led to one of my strongest teammates throwing in the towel and calling it quits. By all rights, if one of us were going to succeed, I would have put my money on him rather than me. It's impossible to truly know what someone else is going through, but he had been faster than me on every recent leg of the journey and I have no doubt he was physically better prepared to summit.

That could have been me, so easily. I could have been on the mountain and ready to summit, but just not found that extra drive. Fortunately, I found the space inside myself to be present and focus only on the next moment of the climb, and I was able to make it to Camp 3 the next day.

TAKEAWAY FOR ENTREPRENEURSHIP

No matter how strong we are, it's easy to become overwhelmed by the journey and let it conquer us. Even the days that are supposed to be easy can quickly devolve. Staying focused and present in the current moment is the only way to accomplish the most difficult sections, one step at a time.

JOURNAL PROMPT

What are the five best pieces of personal or professional news you got in the past week? List them. For each of those events, did you take the time to truly celebrate the achievement? Did you praise and focus on those who were important? Or were you too busy looking ahead to the future?

Happiness and Helping Others Be Resilient

The final version of the happiness hypothesis is that happiness comes from between. Happiness is not something that you can find, acquire, or achieve directly. You have to get the conditions right and then wait. Some of those conditions are within you, such as coherence among the parts and levels of your personality. Other conditions require relationships to things beyond you: Just as plants need sun, water, and good soil to thrive, people need love, work, and a connection to something larger. It is worth striving to get the right relationships between yourself and others, between yourself and your work, and between yourself and something larger than yourself. If you get these relationships right, a sense of purpose and meaning will emerge.

—Jonathan Haidt,
The Happiness Hypothesis:
Finding Modern Truth in Ancient Wisdom

If you were to survey the majority of ancient wisdom on what truly creates happiness in a person, what do you think the lesson would be? It's certainly not riches, as nearly every philosopher and religious tradition agrees. The more money you have, the more you tend to want. Fame doesn't do it either. As with money, the more we achieve, the more we envy those with more.

There are a few different philosophical schools of thought about how to optimize for happiness. Some say that happiness comes from aligning your activities with your passions.[93] Do what you love, follow your bliss, and happiness will follow. Others say that happiness comes from conquering our own needs, our ego.[94] There is a school of thought that happiness comes from the denial of self in the service of others.[95] Indeed, I think there is some truth to each of these notions, and I think of them as different food groups in my well-balanced diet of happiness.

One other component of human happiness that comes up consistently is the idea that happiness comes not from "within" a person but from "between" people, and it is all about the development of relationships and community; happiness is a byproduct of fellowship and belonging.[96]

Unfortunately, the feeling of belonging is strained during the oftentimes lonely entrepreneurial journey. As entrepreneurs and leaders, we feel apart from most of our co-workers. Heavy is the head that wears the crown. We assume our colleagues wouldn't understand our stresses, so we try to protect them from reality.

But it's not just colleagues; being an entrepreneur tends to strain our relationships with family and friends. As we feel the symptoms

---

93 Joseph Campbell, in particular.
94 The Stoics and Buddha focus on removing or overcoming our needs.
95 Christianity, in particular, focuses on fulfillment through service to others, particularly the less fortunate.
96 This is the conclusion Jonathan Haidt reaches in *The Happiness Hypothesis* and similar to what David Brooks reaches in *The Second Mountain*.

of the journey, we tend to turn inward. We become less caring, less kind, less generous, and less giving.

Many times, we aren't aware of these tradeoffs, and we don't see that we are acting selfishly. Other times, we willingly sacrifice our friends and family on the altar of our own ambitions. I hear way too often from entrepreneurs that they think they can be a good husband or a good entrepreneur—but they can't be both. That attitude is completely misguided and breaks my heart.

And so, we set up a false choice by telling ourselves that real entrepreneurs prioritize their businesses above all else. When the business conflicts with friends, family, or relationships, the business should always win.

If research tells us that happiness comes largely from our community with others, and we internalize the false notion that entrepreneurship requires severing the bonds of that community, is it any wonder that entrepreneurs are in such crisis? And given that research shows that teamwork and connectedness to others is critical for survival, effective decision-making, and leadership, is it any surprise that entrepreneurial outcomes are so poor?

When I was growing up, we had a yellowed and worn quote hanging on our refrigerator that I probably saw every single day. It read:

> We flatter those we scarcely know,
> We please the fleeting guest;
> And deal full many a thoughtless blow,
> To those who love us best.
> —Ella Wheeler Wilcox

As entrepreneurs, this is doubly true. We desperately need our team to be there for us and to support us on the journey; we expect much of them, yet we oftentimes find ourselves giving back much less than we should. We show up to family gatherings late, checked out and drained—if we show up at all. We focus inward as a result of the stress and don't ask others about themselves. In our hearts, we mean to be loving and generous people, yet we don't find the time or energy to give or contribute. We don't nurture in the way we want to be nurtured.

The loved ones who make up our support networks will tolerate this selfishness for a while, but their resentment builds. You can't come home to your sanctuary and bring nothing, constantly using up the emotional reserves and labor of the people that love you the most. The walls we don't realize we build to protect ourselves end up forcing away those who are closest to us.

Every bit of survival research reinforces the notion that the people who are most effective in the most difficult situations are the ones who resist the temptation to focus on themselves and instead serve others. Alas, every poorly adapted instinct we have in times of stress tells us to focus inward and ignore everyone else. And so, we push our support networks away the hardest when we need them the most.

Perhaps My Hardest Lesson

As with most of the lessons we've covered, I have lived this one myself. The wound that still stings the most from my entrepreneurial journey was losing my relationship with one of my best friends. Looking back, I failed to recognize a friend in The Death Zone and didn't do enough to support him. I often say that "the tools are useless if the carpenter is having a nervous breakdown," and I'm not proud to say that for a period of time, I focused on the tools—operationalizing the business—at the expense of the carpenter (that is, my friend, the entrepreneur). It certainly didn't help the business, and it cost me a close friendship.

Let me explain. While I was still working at IBM, I had two best friends in Chicago, that I'll call Dale and Nick. The three of us were in our mid-twenties and thick as thieves, hanging out almost every night, talking daily, generally about as close as any group of guys could be. We did everything together.

Dale left IBM and decided, along with Nick, to start a Papa John's pizza franchise in Chicago. There were five equity partners: Dale and Nick each recruited their parents, and I was the fifth. We started off with a bang. We opened on Halloween and proved demand for the product with a line around the block. The excitement was palpable, and while it was far from a sure thing, the financials looked promising. Based on this early success, we decided to go big and grow the company. We were high atop Mount Stupid and already counting the money we just knew was about to roll in.[97]

Unfortunately, even as we were experiencing early success, conflict grew between Dale and Nick's families. I ended up as the mediator, a job that felt important at first, but soon became overwhelming and stressful. I had invested in the company mostly because I thought it seemed like fun, and I didn't want to be left out of what Nick and Dale were building. The two other families were betting more than I was on the business, so this was far more serious and stressful for them.

The company grew and developed over the next couple years. We opened seven stores, but the conflict deepened between the two families. I felt like I was always in the middle, trying to keep the

---

97   Being at the height of Mount Stupid, we weren't even aware that Halloween is the sec-
ond-highest-grossing night of the year for pizza sales behind the Super Bowl.

business from being pulled apart. There were arguments about how much Dale should be paid to run the business, what percentage of time Dale should spend inside the stores, and even how much free pizza each owner should be allowed to order per month. It was crazy.

As the conflicts grew more bitter, I eventually tried to resign my position on the Board. I was far more willing to lose the money I invested than my priceless friendships with Dale and Nick. In hindsight, I wish I had stuck to my guns and walked away, but instead I let myself get talked into staying on.

As the company grew and the stakes got higher, things kept getting more difficult. We expected to be profitable quickly, but rather than taking our profits out of the business, we kept having to invest more to keep the operation afloat. We kept projecting that things would get better financially, but that day never quite seemed to come.

Dale's personal life had taken an even more tragic turn. He had been in a horrific traffic accident that left him badly injured and unsure of whether he would ever walk again. While we rallied at his side in the hospital, and the circumstances brought us together as friends, the financial strain and conflict around the business kept eating away at our personal relationships.

It seemed like a lifeline to me when a larger franchise group offered to buy us out. Dale and I were very ready to sell, but Nick was firmly opposed. He wanted to put together a plan to fix what he saw as the problems with Dale's management and thought he could turn the business into the profitable, cash flowing company we had all hoped it would be when we started. The conflict that had been brewing for years came to a head.

Once again, I was right in the middle of the argument. We needed almost unanimous consent if we were going to sell, and with the families disagreeing, it was a stalemate. I desperately wanted to be out of the entire situation, so at Dale's urging, I twisted Nick's arm. Eventually, I convinced him to ignore his instincts and agree to the sale. I knew it wasn't a perfect outcome, but I was relieved at the thought of the conflict being over and everyone moving on.

Unfortunately, agreeing to the deal doesn't mark the end of the story. It got uglier from there. After we agreed to the deal, it was up to Dale to work through the final process and get the deal closed. During that time, he got very quiet and stopped returning phone calls or emails. Something was clearly wrong.

It got to the point where I had to threaten to get a lawyer involved to just to get him to respond. This was one of my best friends whose hospital bed I stood by for weeks. I was angry, frustrated, disappointed, and just very sad.

By the time the deal closed, it had all boiled over. When we reviewed the paperwork, we realized that a term we had been negotiating was actually a disguised six-figure payout for Dale. We finally understood why he avoided us throughout the closing process. He was enriching himself at our expense! He didn't want to admit that he was taking advantage of his partners.

My heart was broken, but not because of the money. I would have gladly leant Dale anything I had to help him financially. Unfortunately, after we confronted him, there was no denying the fact that he had basically stolen from us.

Worse, I felt like I had been used to manipulate Nick into selling against his better judgment. He had been skeptical all along; I was the one who kept saying we should believe Dale. I felt incredibly naïve and like my trusting nature had been used to defraud my friend.

Looking back on the experience, having processed it for years, my view of the facts hasn't changed much. I still feel the pang of betrayal and still believe Dale acted unethically. But with a bit of age and perhaps some wisdom, I have come to see my role in the tragedy differently and own responsibility for the situation, rather than just thinking of myself as a victim.

I could have been a much more effective Board member. If I had to do it over again, I would have focused my energy solely on Dale. I knew he was struggling, but I didn't have the language or framework to appreciate just how far into The Death Zone he must have been. He was staring down the gauntlet of selling the business he had built from day one and wrapped his identity into. He was going through life-changing physical injuries. It was enough to overcome anyone. Research shows that stresses like these degrade both our decision-making ability and our ethics.[98] None of these things excuse his actions, but they do help explain them.

Worrying about the tactical business questions was a waste of time; every minute spent on those things was a minute not spent trying to support Dale in his Death Zone experience. I use the word "support" very specifically because I don't intend to say the answer was to coddle him. Some of that support could have taken the form of boundaries, guidelines on the negotiation, or other things to protect him from himself. I knew he was going through the hardest set

---

98   Barnes, Christopher M., Schaubroeck, John, Huth, Megan, Ghumman, Sonia, "Lack of Sleep and Unethical Conduct." *Organizational Behavior and Human Decision Processes* Volume 115, Issue 2 (2011): 169-180. https://www.sciencedirect.com/science/article/abs/pii/S0749597811000239.

of circumstances imaginable, and while I tried hard to be a good friend and advisor, I could have done more.

I have come to believe that being surprised when entrepreneurs exhibit bad behavior while they are deep in The Death Zone is like being surprised when a drunk crashes a car. To be clear, driving drunk is a horrible decision, and anyone who gets behind the wheel is culpable for whatever damage they cause. We are all responsible for our actions, even when under duress.

But, as a society, we have also come to understand that it's not exclusively the drunk who bears the blame. The drunk's friends who are more clear-eyed also have a responsibility to take the keys away, to ensure that the drunk doesn't make bad decisions. The bartender has a responsibility to cut someone off who is obviously intoxicated. It's not enough to let the drunk try to drive home and then judge them when they cause an accident.

I let Dale drive the car, and then I complained when he got into an accident.

As entrepreneurs, the team we surround ourselves with will also be going through their own version of the entrepreneurial journey. An obvious example is other entrepreneurs, but there are similar dynamics at play with our senior teams, even our spouses and friends who experience the journey vicariously. In fact, research has shown that both entrepreneurs *and their spouses or partners* take more mental health medications when a business gets launched.[99]

As we become more enlightened and aware of our own mental state, we will also start to notice the effects of the journey in others.

---

99   Dahl, Michael S., Nielsen, Jimmi, Mojtabai, Ramin. "The Effects of Becoming an Entrepreneur on the Use of Psychotropics Among Entrepreneurs and Their Spouses." *Scandinavian Journal of Public Health* (2010): https://journals.sagepub.com/doi/10.1177/1403494 810375490.

Whether they are experiencing their own Delusions of Grandeur or Death Zone, as we begin to develop ourselves, we must look to help our companions as well.

We have all heard the airline takeoff briefing asking you to "put on your oxygen mask first" in case of cabin de-pressurization, and I believe that to be just as true for mental resilience. In order to be good coaches, we first need to be in control of our own emotions. It's also important to be ready to help others with their oxygen masks in the event of an emergency. With Dale, I was blind to the fact that coaching him on tactical decision-making was worthless while his judgment was so impaired by The Death Zone. Giving someone who is thrashing in The Death Zone a finance lesson on balance sheet analysis is like icing the sprained ankle of a patient dying of pneumonia. It may technically help fix a particular malady, but it misses the whole point.

Supporting Others

Remember what I said at the very beginning of the book, to succeed as entrepreneurs we have to stay alive, resist the urge to quit, and keep moving forward? To do that, we need to enable our teammates to do the same thing, one step at a time. We must prepare them, the same as we do ourselves, for the fact that it's going to be a long journey full of difficult moments to be faced head on.

I have learned an interesting lesson talking to people about mental resilience over the past few years. Identifying primarily as an entrepreneur, I saw every lesson through the lens of the entrepreneurial journey. As I read studies about entrepreneurial mental health and became well-versed in the statistics, I came to see entrepreneurs as a uniquely vulnerable and challenged population.

And then I got outside my bubble and realized that everyone around us is going through their own version of the same journey. I talked with the founder of PhD Balance,[100] who told me about the depression and lack of control that PhD students go through in the course of their studies. I talked with single parents and began to understand the challenges of their journey more intimately. I realized that every one of us is answering our own call to adventure in our own specific way. When I was deep in my own Death Zone, I was too myopic and inwardly focused to effectively see or empathize with others. I was so fixated on thinking of my journey as harder that I failed to recognize the parallels.

So, here's a reality check for entrepreneurs. Your struggles are real, no question about it. Your road is hard. But you are also surrounded by people who are facing challenges that are every bit as real to them as yours are to you. Ignoring that fact doesn't mean you are a "committed and focused entrepreneur," it means you are acting like a selfish asshole. I say that with such conviction because I have been there. Unfortunately, I have been the asshole.

If you make a conscious decision to use the journey to nurture the bonds between yourself and others, you'll be a much happier person and an exponentially more effective entrepreneur. Most of the lessons of this book can help others contextualize and cope with where they are in their journey, but I also want to call out four specific ways you can think about helping others to build their mental resilience.

---

100 https://www.phdbalance.com/.

Respect Your Team Enough to Be Honest

Don't insult your team's intelligence by telling them everything is fine when it isn't. Remember how we talked about the skill of discernment, seeing things for what they truly are, being critical to entrepreneurship? Without understanding and facing the true context of the situation, there's no way to effectively prepare, prioritize, or adapt to changing dynamics. This same principle applies to your team: if they are going to face the road ahead of them, they need to understand what is truly there.

If the people you hired are smart enough to be valuable, they are going to be smart enough to sense when things are going wrong. This doesn't mean panic them with every one of the daily ups and downs, but they will adapt to the situation far better if they understand it. No matter how good you think your poker face is, your team probably senses far more than you imagine. Remember that the human mind tends to color in worst case scenarios when there's ambiguity, so chances are that almost anything you say to them will actually be a relief. Also, remember that anxiety is contagious, and humans are finely attuned to sense danger from one another.

The way that I find the sweet spot between being overly dramatic and being too closed off is to make sure I have processed the emotions and facts of what is happening before I share those thoughts with my team. If I haven't come to terms with whatever I may think about sharing, I risk becoming a conduit that simply channels (and potentially amplifies) in a way that isn't helpful. So I try to make sure I have processed the news, usually by journaling about it or discussing it with a trusted advisor. When I finally feel like I can discuss it without my heart rate jumping, that's usually when it makes sense to discuss the topic at hand.

Model Good Behavior

Somewhere along the way of being an entrepreneur, I decided that my job was to model the behavior of the consummate workaholic. Always on. Always connected. Happy to take meetings at 7 a.m., 7 p.m., or on weekends. I was determined to be in the office as early as possible and as late as possible. I wanted to prove to my team that I was committed, but I also wanted to send the message that they should always be working as well.

Looking back, I'm embarrassed. I should have been setting an example of developing mental resilience rather than burnout.

With that in mind, I have evolved my leadership style. I clearly define communication and vacation protocols with my team. I tell them that I check email on my schedule and when it's convenient, usually every two to four hours during the workday and once in the evening. I check Slack on occasion. If something is important, they are expected to pick up the phone and call or text me; in those instances, I try to respond as quickly as possible, but I won't always be on.

I'm no longer embarrassed to take days off, feeling like I'm betraying some sacred oath by putting work on hold. Nor do I work through vacation. Once again, I tell my team that I'm taking time off and won't be checking email. If I'm still "on the grid," I'll let them know that I expect I can return calls or texts within twenty-four hours for urgent and important situations.

Be Vulnerable

I used to think that the trick to projecting strength was to never let anyone see you being vulnerable. Experience has taught me that the opposite is true—trying to project invulnerability is a lie that others see through. People respect you far more if you can honestly let them know that you are vulnerable and hurt but strong enough to continue. Our humanity as leaders makes us more relatable, not less. Acknowledging fear, frustration, or other difficult emotions sets a tone for how your team can process those feelings and continue the journey in a much more sustainable way.

I now share my thoughts and experiences with my teams much more than I used to. I am now forthcoming with them that I see a therapist regularly, and I encourage them to do the same. I let them know when I'm not at my best because I'm exhausted, frustrated, or at my wits end. If I didn't get a full night's sleep because my infant daughter was up all night crying, I tell my team I'm running on fumes and might be a bit shorter than I intend.

That doesn't mean I dump an emotional load on everyone else or make my problems theirs. It certainly doesn't eliminate my responsibility to act like an adult and moderate my emotions accordingly. And, sure, sometimes I need to bring my "A" game even when I'm not feeling my best—that's part of life. But honestly assessing myself for how I'm doing and articulating that where it's useful to the people I work with helps all of us be more effective together. I find that in being honest, we are more willing to give each other the grace we might need that day.

Explicitly Discuss Mental Health and Resiliency

The most direct way to pierce the stigma of mental health and resiliency with your team is to have an explicit discussion on the topic. I love to have my team read books on a variety of topics and then discuss as a team. I find it helps us grow in different ways and get to know more about each other. *Daring Greatly* by Brené Brown, *Reboot* by Jerry Colona, and *Deep Survival* by Lawrence Gonzales are all very readable books that can help drive these kinds of conversations.

There are also organizations that can facilitate these sorts of discussions. Hope for The Day is a Chicago-based nonprofit that calibrates curriculum to the unique nature of your industry, company, and culture, and will lead an education and discussion of mental health for your organization. Their motto, "It's okay not to be okay," is critical for us to make sure our teams understand. It's okay to have a horrible day. It's okay to be stressed to the max. It's okay to need help.

LESSON FROM MOUNT EVEREST

One stupid decision, prioritizing my pride instead of rationally analyzing the risk of my climb, came *this close* to costing me the opportunity to summit, and were it not for the team around me, I would have turned around just before reaching the summit.

One of the most important decisions you make when climbing the mountain is how much oxygen you'll need to make it up to the top and back down safely. Above 26,000 feet is known as The Death Zone because the lack of oxygen causes the tissues in your body to break down. You are slowly dying. And while certain superhuman freaks of nature climb the world's highest mountains without supplemental oxygen, doing so comes with tremendous risk. Climbers without supplemental oxygen account for about 3 percent of the summits and 22 percent of the deaths above 26,000 feet.[101] In mountaineering lore, those people who climb without oxygen are deified as the gods of the sport, and the impressiveness of

---

101   Berkowitz, Bonnie, Cai, Weiyi. "What It's Like to Climb Mount Everest Without Oxygen." *Independent.* May 23, 2016. https://www.independent.co.uk/news/world/asia/mount-everest-what-its-like-to-climb-without-oxygen-a7044021.html.

summitting is reduced in proportion to the amount of extra oxygen the climber requires.

When I made the decision to climb Everest, I knew I was going to use supplemental oxygen (even *my* hubris has its limits), but there was a question of "how much?" The standard amount for the group I went with allowed me to climb at a flow of three liters of oxygen per minute, but IMG offered an option for an additional bottle to be brought up the mountain at a cost of about $7,000.[102]

I declined that option without even thinking too much about it. Some small part probably had to do with the fact that $7,000 is a lot of money, but truth be told, I could have afforded it. I was taking three months off of work, spending the bulk of my life savings, and generally putting everything I had into this trip. I think the reason I declined the extra bottle was ego, the desire to not take any shortcuts or feel like I needed special accommodations made on my behalf. If the "standard" had included the additional bottle, I'm sure I would have gone with that. I wasn't really doing a rational risk analysis, but I wanted the "real" climb, not a more comfortable adaptation.

For some reason, as I declined the extra bottle, the most obvious benefit of the extra oxygen didn't occur to me. I have read more than twenty books on Everest, and in almost every one of them, the climbers who either fail to summit or die do so because they run out of oxygen. Period. It's that simple. And yet, I was focused on some ephemeral idea that I wanted the "real" experience of climbing the mountain and didn't want to make it easier by upping my oxygen *flow*. I was only thinking about more oxygen as a way to adjust my flow, not the duration it would last. It never occurred to me that

---

102 For reference, the entire trip cost about $75,000.

I could simply climb on the standard flow but still have an extra bottle to give me more margin for error in The Death Zone should circumstances outside of my control slow me down.

I have no idea why my brain never made that particular connection. Looking back, it's so blatantly obvious that I still can't explain that blind spot. But, as Orwell said, "To see what's in front of one's nose requires constant effort." I wasn't seeing the thing right in front of my nose.

That connection finally became clear as I reached the South Summit. I was climbing more slowly than I expected due to a combination of weeks of stomach distress and a herniated disc in my back that made every step painful. I got to the South Summit about thirty minutes behind schedule but climbing steadily, thinking I was in good shape. I could see the summit; it felt like I could almost reach out and touch it, and my spirits soared.

The South Summit was the final check-in with my Sherpa and with Base Camp over the radio before we pushed for the true summit. As my Sherpa, Mingma Sona, checked my oxygen bottle, he signaled to me that we needed to turn around and go down, that I didn't have enough oxygen to go on.

I felt like I had been punched in the gut. In that moment, I would have given every dollar I had for one more bottle of oxygen. I was so close. What I hadn't been able to see before became clear to me—the part of my ego that wouldn't let me buy another oxygen bottle would be the thing that would keep me from accomplishing my goal. I was heartbroken I wouldn't make it to the very top and furious with myself for committing such an obvious and avoidable mistake.

I was saved from the consequences of that particular mistake, just barely, when we got on the radio with Base Camp. While Mingma Sona was making the decision on the mountain for us, our group's climbing protocol dictated that Base Camp would make the final go or no-go decisions. They were monitoring climbing speed, oxygen levels, weather, and a variety of other variables. By their reckoning, I was just barely in the safe zone for my final push, and I got the go ahead from our capable and experienced leader Greg Vernovage. He signed off, wishing me good luck, and with a stern reminder not to dawdle.

I got lucky. I managed to make it to the top by the slimmest of safety margins. All of that could have been avoided if I had spent just a few more minutes considering how to maximize my longevity in The Death Zone and increasing my resilience to bad luck by buying one more bottle of oxygen.

TAKEAWAY FOR ENTREPRENEURSHIP

Capital is your oxygen. With more oxygen, the human body can move faster, and with more capital, a company can execute more quickly. Thinking of capital primarily as an accelerant misses the point; it's more important function is that it allows the company to survive much longer when things don't go according to plan. Raise capital when you can, spend it only when you must, and keep as much on hand as possible to mitigate risk and handle contingencies. Learn from my mistakes—have an extra bottle of oxygen in reserve just in case things go wrong.

JOURNAL PROMPT

How do you think the entrepreneurial journey is affecting your team's mental resiliency? Have you broached the topic with them? Have you made your work organization a safe space for your team to share what they are experiencing? How can you improve that?

Reintegration After the Post-Exit Crisis

I won't be in a position to say what you're asking me to say about you until I find out that you died well. You see, someone with vast wealth is no better off than someone who lives from day to day, unless good fortune attends him and sees to it that, when he dies, he dies well and with all his advantages intact.... It is necessary to consider the end of anything, however, and to see how it will turn out, because the god often offers prosperity to men, but then destroys them utterly and completely.

—HERODOTUS,
Histories

When I tell entrepreneurs my stories of pain in The Death Zone, they usually ask me what pulled me out of my dark place. The simple answer to the question is: "exiting the business." Getting out of the game took the acute anxiety off my shoulders. I felt very different when it wasn't on me to make payroll.

But in some ways, after I sold, I felt worse. I was listless, frustrated, lifeless. The best word that I could find to try to describe the feeling is *ennui,* "a feeling of listlessness and dissatisfaction arising from a lack of occupation or excitement." During the last year of SimpleRelevance, I constantly thought, "If I can just get this financial albatross off of me, stop carrying the weight of others' expectations, then I'll be happy." But I was wrong.

In fact, the time after the exit can be *worse*. Without my company to blame my unhappiness on, I had no one left to blame but myself. During my first visit to a therapist in years—after the exit—I confided in her that things should be good in my life, but everything still felt "out of balance."

As with so many feelings accompanying the human journey, Joseph Campbell captures it well:

> As we re-enter the dense, demanding atmosphere of daily life, we can lose sight of the beauty, the mystery and the eloquence of the timeless ways of being expanded; the mythic realm, recently so palpable to us, can feel far away in a hurry. Experiences that were momentous just a few days ago can now seem irrelevant or even somewhat silly in the midst of the day's normal routines. When this happens, we feel ourselves wanting to turn away from our ordinary lives. The appeal and lure of the living myth of adventure pulls at us. We may want to avoid grounding ourselves back into our familiar physical locations in space and boon, not yet having any faith that the boon will now begin to arise from within us, while in the midst of daily life. We may begin to doubt that we can bring forth new life and new love wherever we are presently planted.[103]

---

103 Campbell, Joseph. "The Return Home – Bringing Aliveness Back To Daily Life." Hero's Journey Foundation. https://herosjourneyfoundation.org/blog/return-home-bringing-aliveness-back-daily-life/.

It reminds me of coming down from the top of Everest after summiting. There was no finish line to cross, no cheering crowd to celebrate my accomplishment. A couple Sherpas and climbers gave me a high five. I drank a lukewarm Sprite to celebrate. And then I went back to my tent to rest.

I had no idea my summiting had gone viral back home. Friends and family had been watching my progress over the internet with a satellite tracker and shared the pictures I sent of the summit. In fact, my photo with the iconic Chicago Cubs "W" flag at the top of the world was a minor sensation in Chicago for a few days, with so much hype that when I returned, the Cubs invited me to throw out the first pitch at a game.[104]

But, in that moment, as I got in to Base Camp, there was nothing. No banner, no celebration, no cheering. No one to validate my ego and assure me how impressive I was. I was just a guy, limping into Base Camp, excited to be down from the mountain. I spent ten years preparing and training to climb Everest, ten weeks actually doing it, and ten minutes on top of the world.

It's a funny feeling to focus so much of your life on wanting to do something, whether that's starting a company or climbing a mountain. You prepare and train for it, feeling the fun butterflies at the beginning of the journey. You get into it, find it harder than you expected, and start focusing on the end of the journey. The end of the frustration, the happiness and fulfillment that will come from success. You forget about the moment that you're in and try to take

---

104 Since I know you're wondering, no, the pitch wasn't a strike. But I didn't bounce it, nor did I send it over the catcher's head. I like to describe it as a 12-6 curve just off the plate. You can see a video of the pitch by visiting https://www.facebook.com/NBCSChicago/videos/10155846391131429.

yourself out of the daily grind, living in a future of sunshine and happiness from the successful completion of the journey.

And then you get to the finish, and you're still the same person. Perhaps some extra aches, pains, or scars, but basically still the same. The rewards of success aren't nearly as exciting or interesting as the journey that just reached its conclusion.[105] So, what then?

The Financial Improvement Quickly Loses its Hedonic Value

The primary reason for an exit is usually financial; an exit will either make us rich or at least staunch the bleeding of the company that threatens to make us poorer. While the decision may be emotional or philosophical at the edges, the reason we sell the company is usually about money. And that money usually feels amazing! Whether it is millions of dollars being wired to your account or simply the feeling of being off the hook to make payroll, the freedom that comes with leaving the financial stress of the company behind is real and visceral. It feels like a weight being lifted off the shoulders.

Unfortunately, it's also fleeting. Research shows[106] that when we receive one-time injections of wealth, our minds quickly adjust to our newfound financial situation. We feel great for a brief period of time, but our minds immediately click into the mode of "protecting what we have" rather than the continued gratitude for our

---

105   There's an African proverb that says "If you want to go fast, go alone. If you want to go far, go together." I agree with the quote, but think it misses the even more important point that if you want to truly enjoy the journey and celebrate any successes along the way, it's best to have trusted friends alongside.

106   Diener, Ed, Lucas, Richard E., Scollon, Christie N. "Beyond the Hedonic Treadmill: Revising the Adaptation Theory of Well-Being." Singapore Management University. 2006. https://ink.library.smu.edu.sg/cgi/viewcontent.cgi?article=1920&context=soss_research.

improved situation. If anything, with more to lose, we may find ourselves *more* stressed about money than we felt before.

We don't learn until it's too late, as Nassim Nicholas Taleb writes in the *Black Swan*: "So from a narrowly defined accounting point of view, which I may call here 'hedonic calculus,' it does not pay to shoot for one large win." Unfortunately, entrepreneurship is basically the act of shooting for one large win.

The Feeling of Purpose is Missing

While I was building SimpleRelevance, I never had any question about the purpose of my company. It was to create, to build, to develop technology and applications that were completely new and moved the world forward. As a second order effect, the purpose was to employ people and help build an innovation ecosystem in Chicago. I was purpose and mission driven to the core, with the purpose and mission being all about the need to build.

By the way, as an ancillary effect, the success of SimpleRelevance just happened to increase my theoretical wealth as the primary shareholder and glorify my ego as the face of a successful company. I would have never admitted those latter effects being key motivators (in fact, I would have argued against that reality convincingly). But then I sold SimpleRelevance. All of a sudden, the success of the platform was far less tied to my bank account or ego. All of a sudden, the purpose felt empty and hollow. I was forced to acknowledge my contribution to the world was simply a legacy of more people clicking on more emails and buying more products.

With a little more space and processing, I have come to a different belief about the impact of that journey. SimpleRelevance didn't change the future of machine learning as I had hoped. It didn't fundamentally transform marketing in the way that my grandest visions intended. We did, however, have a lasting impact on most of the people who took the journey, and we created real value for our customers. Long after whatever code we wrote is eventually deprecated, the impact on the humans will remain.

We Become Addicted to the Activity and Our Importance

That ego boost of being needed and inundated with constant activity is real. Feeling constantly needed and active is exhausting—but also gratifying. When we lose the ability to make most of the decisions for our company, it's frustrating to accept the idea that we are not irreplaceable. Especially in the context of building the business where we have pretty much always considered ourselves to be irreplaceable. I have at times, post-exit, had to fight the little golem of schadenfreude in the back of my mind that hopes other people's decisions don't work out so that the new bosses will have to acknowledge just how smart and "right" I was. If you think about the tendency of the entrepreneur to conflate themselves with their business, being told that they are no longer essential to their company becomes an attack on their importance as human beings.

While we are running our business, we can use activity to avoid questioning "why" we are doing what we're doing. And because we oftentimes aren't living in the present but are instead fantasizing about a hypothetical future world where we have exited, are rich, and surrounded by sunshine, rainbows, and unicorns, we are shocked when we get to the finish line and find ourselves feeling like the exact same collection of insecurities wrapped in a lumpy meat-sack of a body. But now we have lost our excuse to ignore all those feelings!

And so, the existential crisis, ironically, is often not surfaced until after the quest.

"Because it's there" feels so much more satisfying as an answer to why we are *going* to climb a mountain than why we *did* climb it.

What's it all for? Why endure the pain and uncertainty? I love how René Daumal articulates the answer:

You cannot stay on the summit forever; you have to come down again. So why bother in the first place? Just this: What is above knows what is below, but what is below does not know what is above. One climbs, one sees. One descends, one sees no longer, but one has seen. There is an art of conducting oneself in the lower regions by the memory of what one saw higher up. When one can no longer see, one can at least still know.[107]

LESSON FROM MOUNT EVEREST

Before going to climb Everest, I did a lot of visualization about how I'd feel on the climb. How would I feel on the days that were hard? How would I feel at the top? I don't remember ever visualizing how I would feel on the way back down the mountain, but if you had asked me, I probably would have said some combination of proud, excited, exhausted, determined to get back down successfully, and so on.

---

107   Daumal, René *Mount Analogue.*

If someone had told me that on the way back to Camp 4 I'd be feeling inadequate and shameful, I would have never believed it. And yet, repelling down the final pitch (known as the Triangle Face) on the way to the safety of Camp 4, there it was. Shame, negativity, the feeling of not being good enough.

You see, I was an hour or two behind the rest of my group, and moving slower than they were. Even now, I feel like I need to list a variety of excuses to you, dear reader, to justify why I was slow. My pride wants me to make sure I reiterate the herniated disc in my back, the fact that I was using less oxygen, and perhaps even my persistent GI distress. Even years later, I'm afraid that you, someone I will most likely never meet, will judge my climb of the highest mountain in the world as "unworthy" because I was behind the pack. Ego is a pernicious thing.

On the Triangle Face, it was even worse. I was angry that I was behind the other climbers. I kept trying to go faster and couldn't. I was frustrated that the rest of my team would be able to go all the way down to the relative comfort of Camp 2 (Advanced Base Camp) while I was too slow and would thus have to spend another night in the "Death Zone" at Camp 4. The only thoughts going through my mind on the way down the Triangle Face were of not being good enough. Being less than I should have been.

At some point, while changing rope lines on the rappel, I snapped out of it. I finally realized the absurdity of that voice and confronted it head on. I stopped for a couple minutes to simply breathe and take in the moment. I said, very definitively to that voice, "I just summited Everest and am safely on my way down, accomplishing a goal of more than ten years. The absurdity of your argument is self-evident, I am good enough, dammit."

I know it sounds silly. It sounds a bit like the character Stuart Smalley from *Saturday Night Live,* "I'm good enough, I'm smart enough, and doggone it, people like me." [108]

But I remember that moment far more vividly than I even remember the summit. I finally had the realization that there was literally no goal I could accomplish that would shut that voice up for even a day. On the way down from the highest mountain in the world, it was still going to yap negativity in my ear. That moment on the Triangle Face might have been the most transformational for me of the entire journey.

When I got home, I got my first tattoo. It's a picture of Everest from a vantage point that clearly shows the Triangle Face. In some ways, I'll admit, the tattoo is a trophy. It's a great conversation starter, "Oh…that? It's a picture of Everest, which I climbed in 2018." But the real reason I got it was the photo of the Triangle Face. It's the reminder to me of finally conquering that voice and the absurdity and the silliness of the feeling of inconsequence and not being good enough.

I try to look at it when I hear that familiar voice of toxic negativity in my ear and remind myself that the voice didn't even think I was good enough while on my way down from my greatest achievement. I remember how that voice tried to rob me of my victory rappel, and that there is no achievement that will quiet the voice. For me, peace only came by acknowledging and confronting that voice in order to silence it.

---

108 PuckMonkey. "Stuart Smalley – Daily Affirmations." YouTube. https://www.youtube.com/watch?v=6ldAQ6Rh5ZI.

TAKEAWAY FOR ENTREPRENEURSHIP

There is no achievement, no amount of fame or fortune, that will silence the voice that always demands more. But that voice, and the shame it brings with it, will make you far less effective as an entrepreneur if you don't learn how to confront it.

JOURNAL PROMPT

Think through three different dimensions of a Venn diagram:[109]
- What do you enjoy doing?
- What do you think you're really good at?
- What makes the world a better place?

Is there anything at the center of these three circles in the Venn diagram? The activities that fall in the center of those three circles are likely to be the ones that are most sustainable and most fulfilling, the ones less dependent upon material success for happiness.[110]

---

109 Two useful resources to explore this in more detail. Designing Your Life: How to Build a Well-Lived, Joyful Life by Bill Burnett and Dave Evans as well as the Hive Global Leadership Program where I went through this exercise. You can find more information about Hive at: https://www.hive.org/.

110 There is a much more comprehensive version of this exercise available from the Hive community for entrepreneurs at https://www.hive.org/resources/ listed under "Designing Your Life Workbook."

If I Lose My Anxiety, Will I Lose My Superpower?

Behind every driven entrepreneur is an eight-year-old desperate for his parent's approval.

—MATT McCALL

"Erik, all this calmness sounds great, but if I lose my drive to succeed, will I lose my superpower? The thing that drives me to outwork everyone else and allows me to win?"[111]

Almost every entrepreneur asks me some version of that same question; it is the single most common topic entrepreneurs bring up after I talk with them. There's an even more honest version of this question that a couple students have asked me:

"Is this calmness thing a luxury of the rich or successful? If you had adopted all this stuff earlier, would you have still accomplished the things you have accomplished?"

---

111   Much of this chapter (and this book in general) has been inspired by my conversations with a mentor, Matt McCall. I'd suggest you also read his thoughts on the topic https://somethingventured.com/2020/02/if-i-lose-my-fear-do-i-lose-my-drive/.

I have thought deeply about these questions and believe that it's not only possible but far more likely for an entrepreneur to succeed by learning the lessons of mental resilience. But, I also know that burden can be a hard one to willingly put down.

From a young age, I identified that I had a willingness to postpone reward and endure pain far more than other kids around me. You may have heard of Walter Mischel's marshmallow test as a way to predict future achievement.[112] The idea is that you put marshmallows in front of kids and tell them if they resist eating them, they'll get twice as many in an hour. I know I would have scored highly on the marshmallow test; I probably would have taken the marshmallow and tried to plant them in the ground, in hopes of growing a marshmallow tree to create returns with interest over time. I was always focused not on the short term, but on the longer journey.

As I grew older and took a job at IBM, I was fond of saying that I couldn't guarantee I was smarter than my peers, but I could certainly control my willingness to outwork them. I took great pains to make sure none of the executives ever saw me coming into the office or leaving it. I had to be there before them and leave after they did.

Pain is for the weak, while pride is eternal. Pain is just weakness leaving the body. You name a meathead mantra that celebrates suffering, and I have probably repeated it. A lot. And the anxiety is a damn good motivator! Most of us, as entrepreneurs, value our ability to outwork our peers. The alternative sometimes feels like a resigned mediocrity. Like taking the Blue Pill in *The Matrix*, ignoring our talents, and living an ordinary and unfulfilling life.

---

112 Mischel, Walter, Ayduk, Ozlem, Berman, Marc G., Casey, B.J., Gotlib, Ian H., Jonides, John, Kross, Ethan, Teslovich, Theresa, Wilson, Nicole L., Zayas, Vivian, Shoda, Yuichi. "'Willpower' Over the Life Span: Decomposing Self-Regulation." *Social Cognitive and Affective Neuroscience*, Volume 6, Issue 2 (2011): 252-256.https://academic.oup.com/scan/article/6/2/252/1619382.

We know we don't want that kind of a life. While we will openly acknowledge that fact, most of us probably wouldn't recognize nor say out loud that some combination of fear and anxiety provides the fuel for our ability to outperform. We recognize that we have this superpower, something that makes us different, but we probably don't stop to spend a lot of time questioning why. In fact, we generally view it as a positive trait, something that usually leads to success. It's only when someone suggests, "Let's be more mindful and reduce some of that fear and anxiety," that some part of us resists. "Wait, I like being an overachiever! I like accomplishing things. I'm not sure I want that part of me to go away!"

And there's good reason to wrestle with this question. We talk about our minds as though the cortex is always right, and our emotional brain is always wrong. In fact, there is an underappreciated amount of wisdom in our limbic system. These get described as "gut" feelings, or something we feel in our "bones." Our limbic systems pick up on important things far faster than our Philosopher brain does. Remember the story of Scott almost being bitten by a snake? We don't want to lose that reflex.

What we didn't talk about in that chapter is even in chronic situations, our Crocodile brain may appreciate what our Philosopher brain misses. Often it's that innate, emotional drive that causes us to leave far more lucrative professions to get into entrepreneurship in the first place! Most Philosopher brain-driven risk/benefit analysis says that being an entrepreneur is an act of near insanity, but we go down the road anyway. The Crocodile brain is usually screaming at us for a reason! And it's going to keep making noise—no matter your efforts to calm it down—until we recognize it.

At its heart, that's why I write and talk about these concepts in the context of "resiliency" rather than "wellness." Implicit in many discussions of "wellness" is the idea that you need to cut back or reduce that drive in order to stay healthy. I generally reject that as a false choice. You may have been told by a doctor to "reduce stress;" you probably haven't been told to develop your mental resiliency to better cope with and adjust to stress. I think "stillness" is critical, but I think it enables achievement rather than slowing it.

I learned this lesson the hard way when I decided I wanted to do an Ironman triathlon. When I first decided I would do it, I was about forty pounds overweight and could barely run a few miles. I had certainly never been confused with an endurance athlete and didn't consider myself to be one. I spent eighteen months with my only defining notion being "I'll outwork everyone else." I didn't value balance. I didn't do yoga, or cross train, or any of that "hippie shit." For me, the equation was easy. "I am going to do an Ironman. That requires a lot of running, biking, and swimming, so I just need to practice running, biking, and swimming as much as is humanly possible, and eventually I'll be an Ironman."

Guess what? It worked! Yes, I got sick a lot. Yes, I was in a tremendous amount of physical pain. I exhibited every symptom of a body being "over trained," which I just chalked up to "weakness leaving the body." If I was tired, that meant I needed to train harder to get stronger. If I felt good, that meant I hadn't been training hard enough, so I needed to pick up the pace. The answer for everything was to "train harder!" And again, to be clear, it worked. I accomplished my goal.

At the Ironman race, I chatted with some of the more experienced athletes about what to expect in the race ahead, triathlon training, that kind of stuff. One of them asked me if I was happy to be done interval training. I didn't even know what that meant! Worse, I ran my first marathon two weeks prior to the Ironman. If you're not aghast at that last sentence, let me just tell you, that's a really, really dumb thing to do. It takes the body at least a month to recover from a marathon, more if it's your first one. I was starting my first Ironman already depleted.

When I finally finished the Ironman, I was on fumes. I could hardly walk; everything was in excruciating pain. My body pretty much always runs warm (I had more issues with heat on Everest than I did cold), but I was freezing cold non-stop for the next three weeks as my body tried to recover.

Those pre-race conversations opened my eyes to the fact that I had not trained intelligently, and a couple years later, I decided to try again. This time I'd be smarter. I would cross train. I would stretch and do mobility exercises.[113] I'd focus more on being smart about training rather than simply "always train more." I hadn't lost my drive (I was going to do another Ironman after all), but I was channeling it and being more intelligent.

I trained less, but smarter. I hurt less and put my body through much less stress. I finished the race, about two *hours* faster than my first race (despite worse weather conditions) and felt so good that I went to the bar with my friends that night to celebrate.

I found the same thing in entrepreneurship. My "grind it out, tough it out, overcome all pain" worked to a point. It helped me achieve some amazing things! But when it broke, it broke catastrophically and left me ill-prepared for the consequences. I outworked most entrepreneurs, but I made bad decisions. Much like my first Ironman, all that pain I put myself through was counterproductive. What I thought was my superpower, the thing that was fueling my drive, was also blinding me to what I needed to understand to maximize my odds of success.

---

113 Two great resources if you find yourself contemplating triathlons. Joe Friel, *The Triathlete's Training Bible* and Kelly Starrett, *Becoming a Supple Leopard.*

Learning to understand and manage our fear and anxiety doesn't rob us of our superpowers. Living a more well-rounded and fulfilling life doesn't make us lazy or doom us to the Rooseveltian idea of being a "cold and timid soul who knows neither victory nor defeat."

The superpower remains. Trust me. I'm not writing this book because I have lost my drive; I'm writing it because I hope to change the world. Not in a superficial sense, but in the very real sense that I hope I can make thousands of entrepreneurs more likely to succeed. I hope I can help them be happier and more fulfilled. And while a compelling case could probably be made to "trade off" hard work for a happier life, there is no trade off at all. When you let go of anxiety and improve your mental resilience, you increase your odds of the very real, very tangible success in your ambitions, while also improving your quality of life and reducing your risks.

The fear that learning these skills will rob you of a superpower is the nagging last gasp of the ego. None of this reduces drive and motivation; instead, that motivation becomes clearer and more sustainable. It's like having a meal with a healthy amount of protein and fat rather than relying on all carbs for energy. Carbs work for energy! And in fact, they are often very useful for it. But developing the balance only improves your ability to do great things.

Learning to understand and ultimately confront that anxiety has made me much more effective in trying to achieve my ambitions. I am far more efficient with my energy. I no longer waste so much time on pointless tasks that make me feel busy. I don't get as worked up about issues that turn out to be trivial. I still burn with ambition. I see a world full of problems I would like to solve, but I am also more realistic about the problems that I can control and thoughtful about how to achieve my desired impact.

There are more literal and figurative mountains for me to climb in my future. It's not that my ambitions have been tempered, but rather that I am pursuing them from a place that has much more peace. Developing the mental and emotional tools in this book helped me face my own demons. My amazing girlfriend, who was critical to coaching me in my darkest times on Everest, became my loving wife. We have built a relationship on a stable foundation of mutual respect. My life is now full of joy. I am now able to appreciate the moments of the journey rather than speeding through them in anticipation of the next milestone. I surround myself with a community of loving family and friends who help keep me both grounded and happy. I am far more peaceful and content.

I don't fear the dark places of my mind anymore. The idea that throwing myself in front of the El train might bring the sweet relief of darkness seems foreign. I remember the feeling in my bones, but it doesn't resonate anymore. I still love to exercise, but I treat my body like it belongs to someone I love, no longer punishing it by demanding it endure endless miles and then cursing it for wanting rest. I mix ample rest and recovery into my regimen, and sometimes, I even let myself skip workouts just because I feel like sleeping more or enjoying an extra couple of hours with my family. I still love to drink a Maker's Mark with my friends, but I rarely find myself drinking to turn my mind off or to self-medicate my anxieties away.[114]

---

114 During the challenging early period of COVID quarantine, I did start to feel that pick back up. The sense of anxiety started to build. But rather than resisting or judging myself for those feelings, I did a much better job of recognizing the anxiety, accepting it, and ultimately letting it go. I discussed the anxiety with my therapist. I wrote about the feelings in a journal. Developing and maintaining a mental resilience practice doesn't make all these feelings completely go away, but it does give us better tools to adapt when they arise.

This doesn't mean that everything is perfect, or that I always respond in each moment exactly as I should. But I have surrounded myself with a support network that helps me recalibrate before things go off the rails. I have developed a habit of meditating and journaling. My wife is quick to make me feel safe and then to help me work through my issues. My therapist helps me reorient myself regularly.

Understanding where you are in the journey and the psychic disconnect between the Delusions of Grandeur and The Death Zone of Imposter Syndrome allows you to orient yourself. Then you can better contextualize and understand what's happening inside your body and how those things present as symptoms in your life. Learning the skills of the great survivors—how to prepare, prioritize, and adapt—equips you to be more effective throughout the journey. Developing the more fundamental abilities of discernment, self-forgiveness, stillness, and presence will unlock those skills and be a force multiplier for your decision-making.

I hope you find the same results I did. A little less anxiety and fewer sleepless nights. More contentment, balance, and happiness. I hope all of those things will come, and they will come in the service of helping you dare greatly. May these tools help you accomplish more, and use your talent and innovation to make the world a better place.

LESSON FROM MOUNT EVEREST

The anxiety and yearning to prove what I'm made of undoubtedly contributed to the reason why I went to Everest in the first place. But it was only through conquering those anxieties and my insecurities that I was able to make it to the top of the world.

At the beginning of the book, I shared the "Why I Climb" poem that I wrote before my trip. I wrote what I knew at the time was a bit of a pretentious sentence, but I felt like it was the most concise way to express a really complex thought:

Hubris may be a catalyst for bildungsroman but is ultimately its antithesis.

If anyone reading this book is an aspiring writer, I'll suggest that you never pen a sentence as obnoxious as that one. I actually put "hubris," "bildungsroman," and "antithesis" into a single sentence! The pretentiousness drips off the page.

But while I may be embarrassed about the word choice, I stand by the idea I was trying to get across. Even before I left, I recognized that arrogance may have been the thing that initially spurred me to believe I could climb Everest. I also realized that only by humbling myself would I actually be able to get to the top. Somehow I knew the lesson the mountain would teach me, even if I had no idea how it would eventually unfold.

I started my journey to Everest from a position of arrogance. I wanted to "conquer" the mountain. I wanted to prove I was "good enough." I wanted to test myself against one of the hardest challenges imaginable. I wanted to be a "real man," as if I even knew what that really meant.

The journey taught me just how ridiculous those notions were. I didn't conquer the mountain; she let me climb her, and she blessed me with the opportunity to get to the top. I didn't get to the top because I was strong enough. She only let me climb her after I had conquered my own demons. I learned humility where I had previously had Delusions of Grandeur. I learned to access true self-confidence in the midst of Imposter Syndrome. I always had the ability to grind hard, but I had to learn to see what was there, to rest, to be present in the journey and to forgive myself my failings. I had to learn resilience and adopt the persona of a survivor.

My demons may have driven me to the mountain, but only through overcoming them was I able to make it to the top.

It may be your demons that pushed you to be an entrepreneur in the first place, but learning to overcome those demons is the only way for you to accomplish what you ultimately are seeking and find peace in the journey.

TAKEAWAY FOR ENTREPRENEURSHIP

Not conquering my anxiety led me to bad decisions and bad outcomes. Conquering it led me to the top of the world. I hope others find a similar experience through the journey.

JOURNAL PROMPT

What anxieties or feelings of "not being good enough" might have influenced your desire to begin this journey? How might those feelings handicap you from succeeding?

BIBLIOGRAPHY

BOOKS & LITERARY WORKS

Aurelius, Marcus, A. S. L. Farquharson, and John Sellars. *Meditations.* London: Macmillan Collector's Library, 2020.

Brooks, David. *The Second Mountain: The Quest for a Moral Life.* Random House Large Print Publishing, 2019.

Brown, Brené. *Daring Greatly: How the Courage to Be Vulnerable Transforms the Way We Live, Love, Parent, and Lead.* London: Penguin Life, 2015.

Campbell, Joseph. *The Hero with a Thousand Faces.* Princeton (N.J.): Princeton University Press, 1968.

Christensen, Clayton M., James Allworth, and Karen Dillon. *How Will You Measure Your Life?* London: HarperCollins Publishers, 2012.

Cohen, David G., and Brad Feld. *Do More Faster: TechStars Lessons to Accelerate Your Startup.* Hoboken, NJ: John Wiley & Sons, Inc., 2019.

Colonna, Jerry. *Reboot: Leadership and the Art of Growing Up.* New York, NY: HarperBusiness, 2019.

Darwin, Charles. *The Descent of Man and Selection in Relation to Sex.* New York: A.L. Burt, n.d.

Daumal, René, and Roger Shattuck. *Mount Analogue: a Novel of Symbolically Authentic Non-Euclidean Adventures in Mountain Climbing.* Cambridge, MA: Exact Change, 2019.

Dhammapada. New York: Oxford U Press, 1936.

Epictetus, and W. A. Oldfather. *Epictetus: the Discourses as Reported by Arrian, the Manual, and Fragments*. Cambridge, MA: Harvard University Press, London, 1979.

Feld, Brad, and Jason Mendelson. *Venture Deals: Be Smarter than Your Lawyer and Venture Capitalist*. Hoboken, NJ: Wiley, 2016.

Friel, Joe. *The Triathlete's Training Bible: a Complete Training Guide for the Competitive Multisport Athlete*. Boulder, CO: Velo Press, 1998.

Gartner, John D. *The Hypomanic Edge: The Link Between (A Little) Craziness and (A Lot of) Success in America*. New York: Simon & Schuster. 2005.

Gonzales, Laurence. *Deep Survival: Who Lives, Who Dies, and Why: True Stories of Miraculous Endurance and Sudden Death*. New York: W.W. Norton & Company, 2017.

Gray, Thomas. *Ode on a Distant Prospect of Eton College*. Oxford, Clarendon Press, 1924.

Haidt, Jonathan. *The Happiness Hypothesis: Finding Modern Truth in Ancient Wisdom*. New York (NY): Basic Books, 2006.

Hanson, Rick, and Richard Mendius. *Buddha's Brain: the Practical Neuroscience of Happiness, Love & Wisdom*. Oakland, CA: New Harbinger Publications, 2009.

HBR's 10 Must Reads on Mental Toughness. Boston, MA: Harvard Business Review, 2018.

Herodotus, Henry Cary, and Basil L. Gildersleeve. *The Histories of Herodotus*. London: Forgotten Books, 2017.

Hesse, Hermann. *Siddhartha*. Vachendorf: Re-Image Publishing, 2017.

Hoff, Benjamin, and Ernest H. Shepard. *The Tao of Pooh: the Principles of Taoism Demonstrated by Winnie-the-Pooh*. London: Egmont, 2019.

Horowitz, Ben. *The Hard Thing about Hard Things: Building a Business When There Are No Easy Answers*. New York, NY: HarperBusiness, an imprint of HarperCollins Publishers, 2014.

Kahneman, Daniel. *Thinking, Fast and Slow*. New York: Farrar, Straus and Giroux, 2015.

Kraemer, Harry M. Jansen Jr. *From Values to Action: The Four Principles of Values-Based Leadership*. Jossey-Bass, 2011.

Krakauer, Jon. *Into Thin Air: a Personal Account of the Mount Everest Disaster*. New York: Anchor Books, 2009.

Langshur, Eric, and Nathaniel J. Klemp. *Start Here: Master the Lifelong Habit of Wellbeing*. New York: North Star Way, 2016.

Martínez, Antonio García. *Chaos Monkeys: Obscene Fortune and Random Failure in Silicon Valley*. New York: Harper, 2018.

Moore, Christopher. *Coyote Blue*. United States: Paw Prints, 2009.

Moore, Christopher. *Lamb: the Gospel According to Biff, Christ's Childhood Pal*. Place of publication not identified: HarperCollins e-books, 2009.

Nietzsche, Friedrich, and Walter Kaufmann. *Beyond Good and Evil: Prelude to a Philosophy of the Future*. New York: Vintage Books, 1966.

O'Loughlin, Sheryl, and Steven G. Blank. *Killing It: an Entrepreneur's Guide to Keeping Your Head without Losing Your Heart*. New York, NY: Harper Business, 2016.

Orwell, George. "In Front of Your Nose." Essay. In *The Collected Essays, Journalism and Letters of George Orwell*. London: Penguin Books, 1970.

Pirsig, Robert M. *Zen and the Art of Motorcycle Maintenance: an Inquiry into Values*. New York: HarperTorch, 2006.

Roberts, David, and Ed Viesturs. *No Shortcuts to the Top Climbing the World's 14 Highest Peaks*. Paw Prints, 2008.

Russell, Bertrand. "The Triumph of Stupidity." Essay. In *Mortals and Others: American Essays 1931-1935*. London: Routledge, 2009.

Rūmī, Jalāl al-Dīn, and Peter Washington. "A Community of Spirit." Essay. In *Rumi: Poems*. New York: Alfred A. Knopf, 2006.

Seneca, Lucius Annaeus. *On the Shortness of Life*. Oxford: Benediction Classics, 2018.

Siegel, Daniel J. *Mind: a Journey to the Heart of Being Human*. New York: W.W. Norton and Company, 2016.

Starrett, Kelly, and Glen Cordoza. *Becoming a Supple Leopard: the Ultimate Guide to Resolving Pain, Preventing Injury, and Optimizing Athletic Performance*. Las Vegas, NV: Victory Belt Publishing, 2015.

Taleb, Nassim Nicholas. *Antifragile: Things That Gain from Disorder*. New York: Random House, 2016.

Taleb, Nassim Nicholas. *Skin in the Game: Hidden Asymmetries in Daily Life*. New York: Random House, 2020.

Taleb, Nassim Nicholas. *The Black Swan: the Impact of the Highly Improbable*. London: Taylor and Francis, 2017.

Thoreau, Henry David, and Bill McKibben. *Walden*. Boston: Beacon Press, 2004.

Tolle, Eckhart. *The Power of Now: a Guide to Spiritual Enlightenment*. Sydney, NSW: Hachette Australia, 2018.

TSE, LAO. *TAO TE CHING*. Place of publication not identified: EDITORIAL ALMA, 2020.

TZU, SUN. *ART OF WAR*. S.l.: PSI, 2020.

Wilcox, Ella Wheeler. "Life's Scars." Essay. In *A Treasury of Favorite Poems*. New York: Fall River Press, 2017.

Wright, Robert. *Why Buddhism Is True: the Science and Philosophy of Meditation and Enlightenment*. New York: Simon & Schuster, 2018.

Wulf, Andrea. *The Invention of Nature: Alexander Von Humboldt's New World*. New York: Vintage, 2015.

PAPERS

Allis, Ryan. "Slides." Hive. https://www.hive.org/slides/.

Åstebro, T. and P. Thompson. "Entrepreneurs: Jacks of All Trades or Hobos?" *Entrepreneurship & Economics eJournal* (2011): n. pag.

Åstebro, T., Holger Herz, R. Nanda and R. Weber. "Seeking the Roots of Entrepreneurship: Insights from Behavioral Economics." *Journal of Economic Perspectives* 28 (2014): 49-70.

Dahl, Michael S., Jimmi Nielsen, and Ramin Mojtabai. "The Effects of Becoming an Entrepreneur on the Use of Psychotropics among Entrepreneurs and Their Spouses." *Scandinavian Journal of Public Health* 38, no. 8 (2010): 857–63. https://doi.org/10.1177/1403494810375490.

Diener, E., R. Lucas and C. Scollon. "Beyond the hedonic treadmill: revising the adaptation theory of well-being." *The American psychologist* 61 4 (2006): 305-14.

Fairlie, Robert W. and S. Desai. "2019 Early-Stage Entrepreneurship in the United States: National and State Report." *Ewing Marion Kauffman Foundation Research Paper Series*(2020): n. pag.

Freeman, MD, Michael A., Sheri L. Johnson, PhD, Paige J. Staudenmaier, and Mackenzie R. Zisser. Ms. *Are Entrepreneurs "Touched with Fire"?* San Francisco, 2015.

Greene, R., S. Hantman, A. Sharabi and Harriet L. Cohen. "Holocaust Survivors: Three Waves of Resilience Research." *Journal of Evidence-Based Social Work* 9 (2012): 481 - 497.

Grossmann, I. and E. Kross. "Exploring Solomon's Paradox: Self-Distancing Eliminates the Self-Other Asymmetry in Wise

Reasoning About Close Relationships in Younger and Older Adults." *Psychological Science* 25 (2014): 1571 - 1580.

Hartmann, R., Anders Dahl Krabbe and A. Spicer. "Towards an Untrepreneurial Economy? The Entrepreneurship Industry and the Rise of the Veblenian Entrepreneur." *Environment for Innovation eJournal* (2019): n. pag.

Hunt, R. and K. Kiefer. "The Entrepreneurship Industry: Influences of the Goods and Services Marketed to Entrepreneurs." *Journal of Small Business Management* 55 (2017): 231 - 255.

Kahneman, D. and A. Tversky. "On the reality of cognitive illusions." *Psychological review* 103 3 (1996): 582-91; discussion 592-6.

Koch, S.. "The risk and return of venture capital Historical return, alpha, beta and individual performance drivers (1983-2009)." (2014).

Kowalski-Trakofler, K., C. Vaught and T. Scharf. "Judgment and decision making under stress: an overview for emergency managers." *International Journal of Emergency Management* 1 (2003): 278.

Kruger, J. and D. Dunning. "Unskilled and unaware of it: how difficulties in recognizing one's own incompetence lead to inflated self-assessments." *Journal of personality and social psychology* 77 6 (1999): 1121-34.

Mischel, W., O. Ayduk, M. Berman, B. Casey, I. Gotlib, J. Jonides, E. Kross, T. Teslovich, N. L. Wilson, V. Zayas and Y. Shoda. "'Willpower' over the life span: decomposing self-regulation." *Social cognitive and affective neuroscience* 6 2 (2011): 252-6 .

Muenster, Marcel, and Paul Hokemeyer. "There Is a Mental Health Crisis in Entrepreneurship. Here's How to Tackle It." World Economic Forum, 2019. https://www.weforum.org/

agenda/2019/03/how-to-tackle-the-mental-health-crisis-in-entrepreneurship/.

Mujica-Parodi, L., H. Strey, B. Frederick, R. Savoy, D. Cox, Yevgeny Botanov, D. Tolkunov, D. Rubin and J. Weber. "Second-Hand Stress: Neurobiological Evidence for a Human Alarm Pheromone." *Nature Precedings* 3 (2008): 1-1.

Pencavel, John. "The Productivity of Working Hours." IZA, April 2014. http://ftp.iza.org/dp8129.pdf.

Richtel, Matt. "The Latest in Military Strategy: Mindfulness." The New York Times. The New York Times, April 5, 2019. https://www.nytimes.com/2019/04/05/health/military-mindfulness-training.html.

Shukitt-Hale, Barbara, and Harris R. Lieberman. "The Effect of Altitude on Cognitive Performance and Mood States." NCBI. Institute of Medicine (US) Committee on Military Nutrition Research, January 1, 1996. https://www.ncbi.nlm.nih.gov/books/NBK232882/.

Siebert, PhD, Al. "Exceptional Mental Health." Al Siebert Resiliency Center. https://resiliencycenter.com/exceptional-mental-health/.

Spivack, April J., A. McKelvie and J. Haynie. "Habitual entrepreneurs: Possible cases of entrepreneurship addiction?" *Journal of Business Venturing* 29 (2014): 651-667.

Swedroe, Larry. "Exposed: The Myth of Private Equity and Venture Capital Outperformance." advisorperspectives.com, 2016. https://www.advisorperspectives.com/articles/2016/07/06/exposed-the-myth-of-private-equity-and-venture-capital-outperformance.

"The Venture Capital Funnel." CB Insights Research. CB Insights, June 5, 2019. https://www.cbinsights.com/research/venture-capital-funnel-2/.

"Why Startups Fail: Top 20 Reasons I CB Insights." CB Insights Research. CB Insights, July 17, 2020. https://www.cbinsights.com/research/startup-failure-reasons-top/.

Wilcox, Ella Wheeler. "Life's Scars." *Frank Leslie's Popular Monthly*, Vol. 42, #4. Oct 1896.

FILMS & TV SHOWS

"Daily Affirmations." Episode. *Saturday Night Live* 16, no. 17, 1991.

Fight Club, 1999.

The Matrix, 1999.

The Pursuit of Happyness, 2006.

"Saved by the Bell." Episode. *Jessie's Song* 2, no. 9, 1990.

The Shawshank Redemption, 1994.

Star Wars: Episode VI – Return of the Jedi, 1983.

Whole. *Parks and Recreation*, 2009.

Whole. *Shark Tank*, 2009.

LINKS & ARTICLES

"Anti Portfolio." Bessemer Venture Partners. https://www.bvp.com/anti-portfolio/.

Anwar, Yasmin. "Mice Resist Cocaine If They Have Stuff to Do." Futurity, January 27, 2017. https://www.futurity.org/mice-addiction-cocaine-959182/.

Bercovici, Jeff. "Why We Need to Talk More About Mental Illness in Tech and Business." Inc.com. Inc., July 7, 2015. https://www.inc.com/jeff-bercovici/austen-heinz.html.

Berkowitz, Bonnie, and Weiyi Cai. "What Happens to Your Body When You Climb Mount Everest." The Independent. Independent Digital News and Media, May 23, 2016. https://www.independent.co.uk/news/world/asia/mount-everest-what-it-s-climb-without-oxygen-a7044021.html.

Bowden, Adley. "VC Investing Still Strong Even as Median Time to Exit Reaches 8.2 Years." VentureBeat, May 19, 2017. https://venturebeat.com/2017/05/19/vc-investing-still-strong-even-as-median-time-to-exit-reaches-8-2-years/.

Carman, Ashley. "This Backpack Has It All: Kevlar, Batteries, and a Federal Investigation." The Verge, March 4, 2020. https://www.theverge.com/2020/3/4/21156136/ibackpack-smart-back-pack-kickstarter-indiegogo-crowdfunding-scam-investiga-tion-ftc-doug-monahan.

dan182. *Jessie Spano Caffeine Pill Freakout! YouTube.* https://www.youtube.com/watch?v=bflYjF90t7c.

"Duration of Suicidal Crises." www.hsph.harvard.edu. Harvard T.H. Chan, March 7, 2017. https://www.hsph.harvard.edu/means-matter/means-matter/duration/.

Gelles, David. "Elon Musk Details 'Excruciating' Personal Toll of Tesla Turmoil." The New York Times, August 17, 2018. https://www.nytimes.com/2018/08/16/business/elon-musk-interview-tesla.html.

Graham, Paul. "Default Alive or Default Dead?," October 2015. http://www.paulgraham.com/aord.html.

Hall, Wayne, and Megan Weier. "Lee Robins' Studies of Heroin Use among US Vietnam Veterans." Wiley Online Library. John Wiley & Sons, Ltd, September 20, 2016. https://onlinelibrary. wiley.com/doi/full/10.1111/add.13584.

Hathaway, Ian. "Time to Exit." Ian Hathaway, January 9, 2019. http://www.ianhathaway.org/blog/2019/1/9/time-to-exit.

Horowitz, Ben. "The Struggle." Andreessen Horowitz, May 27, 2017. https://a16z.com/2012/06/15/the-struggle/.

Horowitz, Ben. "Why I Will Give 100% of My Book Earnings to Women in the Struggle." Andreessen Horowitz, December 21, 2019. https://a16z.com/2014/02/25/why-i-will-give-100-of-my-book-earnings-to-women-in-the-struggle-2/.

"How Long Does It Take a Startup to Exit?" Crunchbase. https://about.crunchbase.com/blog/startup-exit/.

"Ignorance Is Bliss." Dictionary.com. https://www.dictionary.com/browse/ignorance-is-bliss.

"Inspiring Quotes by Ron Swanson of 'Parks and Recreation'." https://www.msn.com/en-us/travel/news/inspiring-quotes-by-ron-swanson-of-parks-and-recreation/vp-AADzgNr.

Jarvis, Alexander. "Uber Pitch Deck to Raise Seed Capital Investment." Alexander Jarvis startup consulting fundraising, pitch deck, entrepreneurs -, October 31, 2019. https://www.alexanderjarvis.com/uber-pitch-deck-raise-seed-capital-investment/.

Knapp, Alex. "Scientists Beat The House At Roulette With Chaos Theory." Forbes. Forbes Magazine, October 27, 2012. https://www.forbes.com/sites/alexknapp/2012/10/27/scientists-beat-the-house-at-roulette-with-chaos-theory/.

"NBC Sports Chicago on Facebook Watch." Facebook Watch. NBC Sports Chicago, June 7, 2018. https://www.facebook.com/NBCSChicago/videos/10155846391131429.

Perry, Adam N, Christel Westenbroek, and Jill B Becker. "The Development of a Preference for Cocaine over Food Identifies Individual Rats with Addiction-like Behaviors." PloS one. Public Library of Science, November 18, 2013. https://www.ncbi.nlm.nih.gov/pmc/articles/PMC3832528/.

"The Return Home - Bringing Aliveness Back To Daily Life." Hero's Journey Foundation, March 2, 2019. https://herosjourneyfoundation.org/blog/return-home-bringing-aliveness-back-daily-life/.

Severinghaus, Erik. "NBC: Raising Seed Money: Lessons Learned from the Middle-School Cafeteria." erik severinghaus, May 14, 2019. https://www.severinghaus.com/new-blog/raising-seed-money-lessons-learned-from-the-middle-school-cafeteria.

Shah, Hiten. "Mint.com Pre-Launch Pitch Deck." SlideShare, January 2, 2010. https://www.slideshare.net/hnshah/mintcom-prelaunch-pitch-deck.

Wilson, Fred. "What A CEO Does." AVC, August 30, 2010. https://avc.com/2010/08/what-a-ceo-does/.

Zhang, Maggie. "The Founder Of FedEx Saved The Company From Bankruptcy With His Blackjack Winnings." Business Insider, July 16, 2014. https://www.businessinsider.com/fedex-saved-from-bankruptcy-with-blackjack-winnings-2014-7.

ORGANIZATIONS

Bessemer Venture Partners. https://www.bvp.com/.
ECONA. https://econa.net/.
"Exceptional Mental Health." Al Siebert Resiliency Center. https://resiliencycenter.com/exceptional-mental-health/.
Founders First System. https://www.foundersfirstsystem.com/.
Hope For The Day. https://www.hftd.org/.

"The Latest from Ethical Systems." Ethical Systems. https://www. ethicalsystems.org/.

National Institute on Alcohol Abuse and Alcoholism (NIAAA). U.S. Department of Health and Human Services. https://www. niaaa.nih.gov/.

National Suicide Prevention Lifeline. https://suicideprevention-lifeline.org/.

Office of the Surgeon General (OSG). HHS.gov, May 14, 2019. https://www.hhs.gov/surgeongeneral/index.html.

"Penn Resilience Program and PERMA™ Workshops." Penn Resilience Program and PERMA™ Workshops | Positive Psychology Center. https://ppc.sas.upenn.edu/services/ penn-resilience-training.

PhD Balance. https://www.phdbalance.com/.

Techstars. https://www.techstars.com/.

Y Combinator. https://www.ycombinator.com/.

APPLICATIONS

Calm, Experience Calm. https://www.calm.com/.

Headspace, Meditation and Sleep Made Simple. https://www.head-space.com/.

Mindfulness Coach. VA Mobile. https://mobile.va.gov/app/ mindfulness-coach.

ACKNOWLEDGMENTS

First and most importantly, none of this would have happened without my amazing wife, Dana. I wouldn't have made it to the top of the world, I wouldn't have gotten this book done, and it wouldn't have been nearly as strong without her edits.

Aaron Houghton, my entrepreneurial partner in crime and constant sounding board for all of these years. I couldn't ask for a better friend and fellow traveler.

Dr. Michael Freeman, who has helped me immensely providing academic and intellectual rigor to my observations as a practitioner.

Matt McCall and Carter Cast, who inspired me to look inward and introduced me to the idea of entrepreneurship as the Hero's Journey.

Ted Zoller and Star Marcello, who generously invited me to speak to their classes year after year.

All of the students at the University of North Carolina and the University of Chicago who listened to and provided feedback on my talks over the years and whose questions have been critical to helping me evolve my understanding of the topic.

Jessica Zweig and Rea Frey, who believed very early on that "I had a book in me" and pushed me mercilessly to refine my story and bring this to the world.

Rachel Beck, my wonderful agent who had the courage to take a chance on a first time writer.

The team at Post Hill Press, especially Debra Englander and Heather King for making this book a reality.

The entire team at IMG, without whom I wouldn't have made it to the top of the world.

Dr. Lisa Andresen and Dr. Adrienne Heinz, who provided endless academic and scientific expertise to the book.

Dan Dal Degan, Allison Stockwell, Michael Seidl, and Mary Volk for reading and providing thoughtful comments and edits.

Shelby Bowers, who worked tirelessly to share the concepts of this book with the world.

And, of course, Ann and Carl Severinghaus, my original investors who have always supported my entrepreneurial spirit.

There's just no way to thank everyone who has been critical along the entrepreneurial path, or making this book a reality. But, to all of you out there, I owe you each a debt of gratitude.